Praise for *Hear Us ⌣ ⋯*

Hear Us Out is listening that honors the dignity and worth of the speakers and their stories. The researchers reflect with curiosity and wonder on the potential of relationship and on how to keep the story alive together—the Sacred Story of hope and love, kept alive for generations through reimagination and the kind of generous connection between stories that we experience in this book. Yoder and her team help us to hear, invite us to connect. They challenge their readers to imagine relationships that nurture stories sacred and personal, lived individually and communally, for the well-being of us all. Not for the survival of the church, but for the well-being of us all—which *is* the story of life.

—Sarah Agnew, storyteller and author of
Embodied Performance:
Mutuality, Embrace, and the Letter to Rome

In a time when so much is changing, leaders are searching for insights to help them navigate the future with confidence. In *Hear Us Out*, we hear from those most affected by the change and most invested in the outcomes: youth and young adults. This book is a much-needed resource to add to the library of those invested in architecting a future faith that matters.

—Rev. Dr. John C. Dorhauer, general minister
and president, United Church of Christ

So many churches are "shrinkling"—shrinking in size and wrinkling with age. They say they want young people to return to the church . . . but do they, really? If there's one book I could recommend for churches to take seriously when they consider ways to welcome emerging generations into their midst, it would be *Hear*

Us Out. It combines quality research with deep reflection and wide affection. Your congregation needs this book, and so do you!

—Brian D. McLaren, author of *Faith
After Doubt* and *Do I Stay Christian?*

If we want to know more about what is happening, or not happening, in our churches, we would do well to listen to those who no longer find church meaningful. This is why you need to read *Hear Us Out*. Sue Pizor Yoder and her colleagues in Co.lab.inq introduce us to the worlds, priorities, anxieties, wounds, and questions of Millennials and Gen Z. Their research and the stories that they have gathered reflect a startling picture of the church. But they also paint a beautiful picture of what the church could be: a place where belonging is at the center of our communities and a meaningful life is possible for everyone.

—David M. Mellott, president, Christian
Theological Seminary, and author of
*Finding Your Way in Seminary:
What to Expect, How to Thrive*

The critical theological question of our age is how we choose to belong to one another. In this age of deep global transformation, our sense of connection defines the boundaries of our courage to change for the better in the face of global warming and geopolitical unrest. In *Hear Us Out*, Sue Pizor Yoder and her colleagues deepen our understanding of what is at stake in this moment of human transformation. It's a compelling call to action to share our stories, co-create a more just world, and take seriously the call to Love we hold at the center of the Christian life.

—Rev. Cameron Trimble, author of *Searching for the Sacred,
60 Days of Faith for Women,* and *Piloting Church*

HEAR
US
OUT

HEAR
US
OUT

SIX QUESTIONS ON
BELONGING AND BELIEF

SUE PIZOR YODER AND CO.LAB.INQ

FORTRESS PRESS
MINNEAPOLIS

HEAR US OUT
Six Questions on Belonging and Belief

All Scripture quotations, unless otherwise indicated, are from the New
Revised Standard Version Bible, copyright © 1989 National Council of the
Churches of Christ in the United States of America. Used by permission.
All rights reserved worldwide.

Library of Congress Control Number 2022058469 (print)

Cover design and illustration: Emily Harris

Print ISBN: 978-1-5064-8919-3
eBook ISBN: 978-1-5064-8920-9

*To our Conversation Partners: We hear
you, and hope we've represented you well.
Thank you for sharing your stories with us.*

*We also dedicate this work to Steve Vulcheff,
Bonnie's late husband, whose loving support
knew no limits, and now rests in beloved memory.*

CONTENTS

PREFACE
A Note from Sue Pizor Yoder

I have never had the desire to write a book alone. At the same time, I have felt a great desire to share the information I have acquired and learned over the years and welcome dialogue with others. So I was thrilled when the opportunity presented itself to author a book with a group of colleagues based upon years of research, study, personal encounters, and experience.

I entered ministry with a passion, a fire even, to engage those "outside" the church. I have been a pastor for almost 40 years, serving over half of those years in actively growing Presbyterian Church (USA) congregations of between 1,600 and 3,500 members. I was invited to serve three fast growing churches where I hoped to do this (each while most churches were in decline). However, what I discovered was that most of the growth occurring in these megachurches was the result of participants' dissatisfaction in their previous churches rather than attracting new people. I felt like our membership increases were the result of people "aquarium jumping" while I wanted to go fishing in the vast blue ocean. Let me be clear: I had *no* desire to convert people. I deeply wanted folks to meet the unconditionally loving, wildly compassionate, undeniably gracious God I had come to know. What to do? I chose to pursue a doctoral degree in the hope that I might discover new thinking, ideas, and possibilities for such engagement.

It became apparent to me throughout my doctoral research that most people who believed in God were outside the church, synagogue, temple, or mosque. In the late 1990s my research had already indicated that two-thirds of people in the US who were open to God were not regularly worshipping in any formal community. As a naturally curious person, I felt compelled to find out why. This curiosity led me to explore the intersection between those who seek to express their religious identity outside the traditional church setting and a community in which that expression is possible. In 2014, I developed a community that intentionally reaches to those outside the church, called The Barn.[1] Many found a safe place to explore God through engaging in this innovative community. Once well established, we transitioned The Barn to new leadership so that I could continue this exploratory work of cultivating a variety of communal spaces for people to creatively engage and express their religious identities. I left The Barn in 2018 to develop a second community called Blank Slate,[2] and continue to serve as its pastor, facilitator, and community leader. Blank Slate offers a variety of ways for people to explore what they believe and ask questions of meaning and importance.

My doctoral research in communication theory, homiletics (preaching), and generational theory led me to several discoveries that informed the development of these innovative communities. With each emerging generation in the US there are fewer and fewer people drawn to institutional religious settings. Each generation that I studied, specifically builders,[3] boomers,[4] and busters (more commonly referred to as Generation X),[5] has its preferred media for communication. Builders favor print media (books, newspapers, newsletters, the Bible), boomers prefer television and common experience, and Gen X engages through interactive digital media. In this unique time in history, three very different modes of communication are available and employed differently by each generation. I cannot overstate the significance of this reality. One reason institutional religious settings are attracting fewer people from emerging generations is because institutions are using older, established communication methods to which younger generations do not relate. The Barn and Blank Slate are two examples of innovative ministries that have been experimenting with a variety of communication methods with noteworthy success: visual arts, multimedia, storytelling, improvisation, technology, various genres of music, and dialogical, and interactive teaching.

Studies show that the institutional church is dying. This was a painful reality for someone who loves and was shaped by that very church. I found myself asking *How, then, are those people not involved in religious institutions being shaped?* I made some interesting discoveries:

- Through planting two new communities, I have become aware that spirituality among the young is alive and well. While they may not relate to the traditional religious institutions, a majority are still quite spiritual. They are open to God, mystery, and exploration in dialogue. However, within churches, growing numbers cite encounters with rigid beliefs, irrelevant dogmas, and out-of-touch orthodox practices. When the church or religious institution fails to offer young adults a safe place to question, doubt, and explore what they believe, emerging generations will seek to have their spiritual needs met elsewhere.

- Generational studies have continued into the rapidly growing generations of millennials and Generation Z. Millennials and Gen Z are growing up in a different world than their predecessors, and encountering religious institutions for themselves. Unfortunately, critique of institutional religious organizations from these emerging generations remains no different than

that of Gen X, and if anything, is much more pointed,
given faith communities' relative lack of adaptability
and innovation in becoming accessible to younger
generations.

I wanted to understand more about this reality. I invited a
group of astute colleagues to join me in my search for understanding. We wanted to explore how those under age 40 are making
meaning. I applied and gratefully received a pastoral study project grant through the Louisville Institute. The core question we
were asking was this: *How are people aged 18–35 who do not affiliate
with any religious tradition exploring and constructing meaning
in community?* In our grant proposal we elaborated: "We would
like to engage with a variety of such persons in collaborative
(storytelling) conversations around truth-seeking and meaning-
making. We believe that learning about their spiritual questions
and yearnings can provide a foundation for understanding and
action for the faith community, as both critique and blessing."

The colleagues I invited to journey with me represent
an amazing group of academics, consultants, pastors, regional
denominational leaders, applied linguists, and storytellers. They
represent Presbyterian, United Church of Christ, Lutheran,
Evangelical Congregational, and Moravian traditions. We also
engaged Episcopal, Methodist, Jewish, and Baptist voices in
conversation.

The team that brings this book to you consists of eight col-
leagues who have truly become great friends through this process.
I count it a privilege to work with each of them: Bonnie Bates,
Brandon Heavner, Joanne Marchetto, Jill Peters, Steve Simmons,
Janet Stahl, and Jim Stahl. Working together has felt like we have
experienced a bit of God's vision of agape love here on earth.
You can read more about each of these amazing humans in the
about the authors section.

Our team created a three-step research proposal. First, we scanned the landscape, creating an extensive bibliography that individual team members divided, read, and summarized for the entire team to consider. We collectively read more than 75 books on a wide spectrum of topics germane to our research: millennials, Gen Z, anatheism, agnosticism, atheism, magic, communication theory, adaptive change and leadership, narcissism, cultural shifts, tribal life, storytelling, oral history, the language of faith, media, evangelicalism, the theology of Harry Potter, and shifts in biblical interpretation to name a few. Additionally, we listened to podcasts, read dozens of articles, and explored blogs and websites surrounding the reasons why so many young people are increasingly nonaffiliated. We studied meaningful secular trends like CrossFit, yoga studios, and humanist chaplains' offices at colleges and universities, as well as imaginative religious communities like Pop-Up Shabbat, the Living School for Action and Contemplation, and Buddhist Geeks. We gathered and reviewed information from our respective denominations. This step in the process provided us with a significant base of quantitative research.

Second, we focused in on key learnings. Having amassed a large amount of information, what rose to the top? What was consistently present in our reading? What questions did we have? What conclusions could we assert? As we discussed, wrestled with, and digested this knowledge, we developed a series of questions that we originally intended to utilize in focus groups; however, the pandemic necessitated that we complete this next step via Zoom. We interviewed a total of 225 people, 200 of them between the ages of 18 and 40, and asked them to respond to five prompts designed to assess whether our "book knowledge" matched the real-life experience of our interviewees. We came to refer to our conversation partners as "nones" and "dones," as they either had no religious affiliation (nones) or they were done with established institutional expressions of faith (dones).

We initially crafted five questions inviting respondents to share their stories about a variety of different topics. These queries were the basis of our ethnographic research. We believed these questions would help us identify how nones and dones felt about and experienced things. These questions were questions of inspiration, belonging, values, adversity, and legacy. However, after interviewing only a handful of people, *our conversation partners requested to tell us about their faith experiences,* so we added a new, sixth prompt on beliefs and practices. We communicated to our partners that we incorporated the last question at the request of their peers who had already been interviewed. At the end of each interview, participants had the opportunity to share anything that they thought would be helpful to our research surrounding how emerging generations are making meaning.

We then contracted with the amazing Marjorie H. Royle, PhD, Interview Transcriber and Data Analyst, to transcribe all the Zoom recordings verbatim and assimilate statistical information from an initial five-minute survey regarding age, education, gender identity, sexual orientation, race/ethnicity, immigrant status, faith traditions of origin, current belief system, and a ranked ordering of current values. After a weekend retreat, every team member reviewed, observed, evaluated, and formed conclusions regarding each of the questions' responses. In addition, team members indicated how their own assumptions and self-evaluations might influence how they read our conversation partners' responses and shared these with the whole team.

Our conversation partners' honesty, insights, openness, and thoughtfulness captivated us throughout the active interviews and as we shared insights from the transcripts. Not one participant refused to answer a question, and most were quite impressed by the questions we asked, stating "This has been really helpful... it's given me a lot to think about... it wasn't what I expected... thank you!" or "I wish I'd had this kind of openness in my faith community growing up... I wouldn't be where I am today."

The research team felt positive about the diversity of our conversation partners. About two-thirds of our partners had some history in the Lehigh Valley of Pennsylvania. The Lehigh Valley is home to 14 colleges and universities. Nine offer four-year undergraduate and/or postgraduate degrees. The Valley has a diverse and thriving arts community. In addition, the community has a wide variety of ethnic diversity, immigrants, faith traditions, and family structures. Among our conversation partners were former or present Christians, Jews, Buddhists, humanists, agnostics, atheists, pagans, universalists, seekers, and searchers. A few of our partners consider themselves to be practicing their religion occasionally, or in recovery from their past belief system.

It is interesting to note that while several conversation partners indicated they were Christian in the survey given at the start of the interview, we discovered through the conversation that very few were actively participating in the Christian faith specified. There are a few reasons we might attribute to this reality. Perhaps this was an answer they thought was *expected* of them before the actual interview began. Maybe this was what they thought *we* wanted to hear. Or they felt obliged to acknowledge the faith of their upbringing in some way. Regardless, we discovered by the end of our conversations that few continued to hold to the religious practice they had identified.

Those interviewed covered a wide educational spectrum, with a generous representation from the LGBTQIA+ community, and a spectrum of white, African/Black, Hispanic/Latinx/Puerto Rican, Asian/Syrian/Nepali, and bi-racial individuals. (Please see Appendix 2 for a further breakdown.) Throughout the book, we will use pseudonyms with an asterisk to indicate the voice of our conversation partners. We tried to select a representative sample of the voices we heard.

It is important to note that we completed each of these steps with the utmost care, maintaining the confidentiality of our conversation partners, thoroughly vetting our own findings and thoughts, wonderments, musings, and conclusions along the way. The team worked collaboratively throughout the entire process, challenging one another's thoughts, agreeing to disagree, and forming ideas upon which we all agreed. We began to refer to ourselves as Co.lab.inq. This name identifies three important values that guided our discussions and the writing of this book:

1. *Co*: Our partners place a high value on working together in teams. One might even say they perceive this as the way of the future. They question a hierarchical approach to leadership. All people expect their voices to have a place and value in conversation. We found immense value in collaborating and not giving one person's voice the final word.

2. *Lab*: We see our work as a lab in which we explore, consider, imagine, lean in, get curious, ask questions, and challenge the ways we have done things historically if they are no longer working. Phyllis Tickle referred to this process as a necessary Great Rummage Sale. We need to ask: *What should stay? What should go since it has fulfilled its purpose? What new things might we need to incorporate or adapt moving forward?* We listened to hear what is important to preserve, and what needs to be recycled. What can someone else use but is no longer useful for us?

3. *Inq*: We "leaned in" to inquire, to try and discover with fresh ears what emerging generations were saying to those of us who represent faith communities. We helped one another remain curious. We asked questions, making very few statements. We tried to be inquisitive instead of dogmatic, relational instead of legalistic, full of wonder and possibility instead of holding on for fear of change.

The third step in our process is before you. Two team members coauthored each chapter, with a third serving as an editor. The entire team then collectively reviewed each chapter draft. So essentially you have the thoughts of eight different people in each chapter! We wanted to draft this book in a way that invited conversation, dialogue, and wonderment. We love the church. How would any religious tradition stay alive over hundreds or thousands of years if it were not for those who raise questions, for those who dare bring forth creative imagination rooted by deep longing?

In addition, our team could not have done its work without the tireless effort of Marge Royle, who singlehandedly transcribed all the interviews and helped us to make sense of a mammoth amount of information. She went above and beyond to accommodate our work in a timely and thoughtful manner. Our editors, Beth Gaede and Laura Gifford, have proven invaluable. They have walked us through this process with patience, expertise, and compassion, and offered much-needed encouragement. We are also indebted to and gratefully acknowledge our grant support from the Louisville Institute. I think I speak for the team when I say that we are grateful to our families, who have graciously given us the time and encouragement needed to engage in this work.

We especially want to thank you, our readers, for joining in this conversation. We welcome your thoughts, feedback, reflections, and input. You can write to us at: Co.lab.inq@gmail.com.

—Sue Pizor Yoder

SO... AN INTRODUCTORY INVITATION

Sue Pizor Yoder, Brandon M. Heavner, & Stephen Simmons, Authors
Jill Peters, Editor

"It's dangerous to go alone! Take this."

—*The Legend of Zelda*

"We did not want to interrogate these folks. We did, however, want to interrogate ourselves."

—Steve Simmons

"The first step to getting anywhere is deciding you're no longer willing to stay where you are."

—Anonymous

So... One of our key observations in over 200 conversations with emerging generations who identify themselves as religious "nones" and "dones" involved the interjectory words they use in casual conversation.[1] Instead of discourse placeholders like *but, um, uh,* or *oh*, we observed emerging generations default to *so*, which is fascinating in and of itself. *So* suggests intent, causality, intensity. *So* gives purpose, qualifies consequence, and offers a frame of reference through which we might develop some type of intimate relationship. *So,* for our conversation partners, is a great unifier because of the way it invites people into a conversational experience that transcends and yet includes personal perspective. *So* invites imagination, wonder, and the vulnerability to explore what might not yet be, now. So... let's start with a story.

SUE'S STORY

When I was about six years old, I had a game-changing encounter with God. I accompanied my mother on a tour to a state institution that "warehoused" persons with disabilities. The institution was relocating and integrating its residents back into local communities as a response to the Civil Rights Act of 1964. While my mother learned about the horrific stories and nightmarish conditions in which unknowable numbers of people with disabilities lived and died, I wandered over to the metal, cage-like crib of a child not yet placed into the community. As I recall, the child had only one arm, no ability to verbalize, and was scarily alone. Trying to make sense of what was happening, I stood perplexed while staring at this child. My eyes caught his and he warmly smiled at me. I sheepishly smiled back and reached my tiny hand to his. We locked eyes and shared a moment that words cannot describe. I heard a voice clearly say, "This is my child whom I love. You love him too." This sent me on a quest to come to know more about the One whose voice I heard and to identify my purpose as one of love.

Fast-forward. I have now been a pastor for almost 40 years. The institutional church that I served for the first 21 years of ministry is in steady decline. Within my own family, I have three adult children, raised in the church, who do not participate as adults. They have joined the ranks of countless others who are leaving institutional religious settings. My doctoral work in the late '90s made clear that two-thirds of people in the US were no longer worshipping in an institutional setting, but many of those same people considered themselves to be spiritual. These realities prompted me, in 2005, to shift my work as a pastor from those primarily inside the walls of traditional churches to those outside its walls. I deeply desired to understand, learn from, and explore the shifts I noticed: from belief to uncertainty, from religious membership to an exploration of spirituality, from practicing faith inside to outside the institution, from monotheistic faith to a bundled spirituality, and from cultural adherence and expectations to cultural rejection/questioning of religious institutions. I wanted to understand these shifts and what led to them.

A. Exploring the Shift

More than a decade later, we can undoubtedly see that the fastest growing religious group in the US is the "nones" and "dones." I am incredibly curious about nones, who indicate they have no religious affiliation, and dones, who desire no part in institutional expressions of faith. Why are most young adults no longer relating to the institutional church? What has changed that might be contributing to this seismic shift? Is it still true that most consider themselves "spiritual" people, and if so, what is the difference? If, for hundreds of years, people answered questions of meaning, purpose, and destiny through belief in God, how are nones and dones now answering these questions? How are those without a faith community in which to grow, interpret, and struggle with questions of faith and life meeting their human need for community? Where do they find a belief structure that guides them? I began reading and asking lots of questions. I quickly realized this task was large and one that would be better served by a team and a variety of perspectives.

In 2018, Co.lab.inq was formed by people who were raised in the church, nurtured by the church, and have engaged in vocations that continue to serve the church, its people, and the communities in which they are involved. We have been meeting, collaborating, and asking questions for over four years. Co.lab.inq serves as a descriptor both of our work together and of what we hope will continue beyond us—a laboratory of collaborative inquiry. We have all dedicated our lives to God's service. We all desire to engage in active conversation about matters of faith and practice. We have all found our faith to be life-giving, life-sustaining, and central to who we are. While we have served our respective institutions, we agree that it is high time we take an open look at its shortcomings. To do this honestly, we had to separate the teaching and practices of the various institutions from the God they intend to serve. Most importantly, we love the church institution enough to speak truth to those committed to it for the sake of its original purpose: to love, serve, and enjoy God and God's creation forever.

To that end, we focused our attention on those who self-identify as nones and dones within emerging generations. We began our exploration by trying to gain all the information about, knowledge of, and appreciation for them that we could. Particularly, we concentrated on millennials, those born between 1981 and 1995, and Gen Z, those born from 1996 to about 2019. We wanted to understand what emerging generations shared in their lived experience. Stereotypes and labels are patronizing and dismissive. At the same time, it is helpful to acknowledge cultural trends and characteristics that a group of people exercise within our society. Below are highlights from two years of reading and research. Our statements are not meant to apply to all within their generation, but to describe general tendencies. The next step was to interview more than 200 people to assess the findings of our reading and research.

In sections B and C, we list the data we accumulated from our literature review.

B. Millennials

- Millennials desire authentic and meaningful relationships. Their circle of friends is typically small, often limited to family, work colleagues, and a few close friends.

- They often possess little confidence in institutions because of things like the war in Iraq, the shift toward national isolationism rather than regional cooperation, and the Catholic Church pedophilia scandal. They are not joiners of clubs or organizations yet will trust someone who represents an institution well (think Bernie Sanders, Jacinda Ardern, Greta Thunberg, George Clooney).

- They are passionate but seldom feel challenged to engage their passions; when presented with an ethical cause, they will deeply invest themselves by taking lower pay or overworking.

- They are suspicious of and disillusioned by our current political system and despair at not being able to change it. They believe it is hopelessly corrupt and deadlocked. As a result, more than one-third are opting out of the two-party system and are broadly libertarian in orientation.[2] In 2016, more people voted for *American Idol* than the president of the United States.[3] They are finding creative workarounds to raise their voices and have them heard.[4]

- They are compassionate, yet they financially give differently than previous generations. They are informed givers, giving through platforms like Venmo, GoFundMe, or directly through social media.

- Millennials prefer an egalitarian, collaborative, shared leadership style. They value process above goals. Ethical objectives and practices are essential for their participation.

- They are flexible in planning, work habits, and their social lives.

- Labeled as lazy by older generations, "uninspired" may be a more accurate description for millennials.

- They value and seek experiences more than material things.

- Their transition to adulthood is generally slower (i.e., getting a driver's license, first job, first relationship, leaving home, bearing children, experimentation with drugs and alcohol). Longer life span, challenging economic conditions, lack of job accessibility, and financial complications like student debt exemplify the circumstances contributing to this phenomenon.[5]

- They are open to exploring and naming their imperfections, shortcomings, and mental health issues. Unafraid to seek help, millennials see these as opportunities for learning and growth. They honor honesty above perfection and see challenges as a part of life and not something to fix and forget.

- Many millennials appear more relationally indefinite or unsure, exercising extreme caution when committing to relationships. Research indicates they delay marriage if they marry at all, will hook up casually, and tend to have fewer, if any, children. They have reservations in exploring committed relationships.

- Millennials can project a false sense of self-confidence, possessing higher than average narcissistic tendencies compared with previous generations. They have grown up receiving constant affirmation and were told they could succeed at anything. They are unsure

of how to transition from school to work and are not
certain who or how to ask for help.[6]

- They are open to innovation and not afraid to try new
things.

- Millennials possess a deep desire to be real and authentic yet recognize that social media platforms are often
the opposite, leading people to "show their best and
hide the rest."

- Simultaneously, they value intergenerational encounters and are open to, and desire relationships with,
older mentors.

- Millennials are increasingly receptive to exploring
awe, magic, wonder, and mystery.

- Millennials are inclusive and comfortable with diversity, yet research reveals they do not often have close
friends of different races, ethnicities, etc.

C. Generation Z

- There is much still to discover about them, as they
are only 10 to 26 years old; they are still discovering
themselves.

- Gen Zers have never known life without a smartphone.
The popularity of iPhones has led some to nickname
this generation "iGen." They often sleep with and
check their phones more than 80 times per day.[7] They
are often sleep deprived as a result and perceive their
phones to be a part of them. They are fluent in all
forms of technology, with a proclivity to multitask.

They expect immediate and rapid responses to queries, a quick and continuous feedback loop.

- While holding strong feelings on social issues, their activism often means clicking "like" on a social media post. Altruism is important, yet they have trouble following through.[8]

- Many express cynicism regarding their capacity to have any impact on politics and government. Independent politically, they lean toward libertarianism. Gen Z is disconnected from, dissatisfied with, and distrustful of government. Concurrently, Gen Z desires government-sponsored services like childcare, healthcare, and college education.

- Statistically they represent the most severe mental health crisis in decades.[9] Their mental health is below average; loneliness and bullying are soaring, especially online; they have the highest suicide, depression, and anxiety rates of any generation on record.[10]

- They are cautious in relationships and fear "ghosting," in which a significant other just stops texting as a way out of the relationship.[11]

- They are often lacking in social skills.[12] The pandemic has only increased this reality.

- Gen Zers, like millennials, tend to grow up more slowly, but are less rebellious; more tolerant, but less happy.[13]

- While research reveals there is a higher-than-average narcissistic tendency among millennials, this is not so among Gen Z. They appear more empathetic, altruistic, and realistic.

- They are seeking a place to belong and to discover a sense of purpose.

- They believe from observing millennials that the work/social balance millennials thought possible is unattainable. Perhaps due to growing up during the Great Recession, little separation exists between work and life. They are returning to the out-of-balance work ethic of the 1990s.[14]

- Gen X, like millennials, anticipates debt and the reality that they will need to work excessive hours just to keep their heads above water. Gen Zers are realistic in accepting that their financial success will be less than that of their parents.[15] They will experience the effects of the exponentially increasing wealth gap.

- Gen Z embodies the maxim *carpe diem*, having grown up amid school shootings, gun violence, the climate crisis, a democracy that is at risk, a global pandemic, and potential global war. There is an increased sense of nihilism.

- Many see Christians through the single lens of what the media presents, which often depicts what outspoken Christians oppose rather than what faith groups believe.

- They are unprecedented in their desire for inclusivity. They celebrate the LGBTQIA+ community, racial diversity, and those differently abled. Interestingly, while they celebrate diversity, their closest friends tend to be people just like them.

- They are more fluid in their thinking and expressions of their gender identity and sexual orientation than previous generations. They are more open to nonbinary orientations to gender.

- The majority are growing up in nonreligious households. The largest religious category among the class of 2019 is agnostic.[16]

D. Emerging Generations

Part of the difficulty with the predominant literature published about religious nones and dones among these emerging generations is that such work often makes this population out to be a project. We prefer to view them as friends with whom we have yet to make an acquaintance. Faith communities have notoriously hosted conversations about how to get "those people" into church, often devolving into lament about athletic events scheduled during prime church-gathering hours. You may have even picked up this book attempting to find the "secret formula" for how to bring young people into your faith communities in the hope that their youthful energy, innovative charisma, and endless amount of free time will be the saving grace for a declining institutional infrastructure.

People are not a project. Nones and dones are fellow humans on a similar journey to get through this thing called life, and in that alone share more in common with active participants from traditional faith communities than most would acknowledge. This is not a study in the quantitative sense, where we have crunched the numbers and synthesized a response to fill up your worship space's pews. This is also not a

This book is primarily an invitation into a process of curiosity, wonder, and meaningful connections with other people.

study where we vilify communities of faith and advise them to be more like an athletic club, yoga studio, or pub crowd. Those studies and suggestions exist elsewhere. We may refer to them as helpful, but this book is primarily an invitation into a process of curiosity, wonder, and meaningful connections with other people.

E. The Lay of the Land

Important on any journey is an understanding of the lay of the land. As Co.lab.inq gathered to discuss how we would approach people to invite them into conversation, it became apparent that our location in Pennsylvania's Lehigh Valley (LV) served as a unique opportunity to glean a snapshot of what religious nones and dones from emerging generations may be experiencing in other geographical settings. Situated as a bedroom community to both New York City and Philadelphia, the LV has major highways connecting it to Washington, DC, and Boston, with corridors to Pittsburgh and regions farther west. It is becoming a hub of economic growth and expansion in the mid-Atlantic region.[17]

Stretching across two counties, the Lehigh Valley encompasses the three primary cities of Allentown, Bethlehem, and Easton (ABE), surrounded by 62 municipalities divided into 17 school districts, making it the 65th largest metropolitan area in the United States. Home to 14 colleges and universities, the LV is seeing growth in various aspects of business, manufacturing, the arts, and health sciences.

Since 2012, the Lehigh Valley has experienced a population growth of more than 10 percent of persons among the 18 to 34 age group, which makes it the fastest growing area for this age group in all of Pennsylvania. During this same time, the LV has experienced a total population growth of 6.2 percent. The LV is becoming increasingly younger, as well as more ethnically diverse.

The 2020 census suggests that every minority population in the LV doubled from 10 years prior, with a 10 percent decline in the white population.

A century ago, Western European immigrants populated the landscape alongside the then booming titan that was Bethlehem Steel. Since 2003, the economy has shifted dramatically from manufacturing giants such as Bethlehem Steel, Ingersoll Rand, and Western Electric/Bell Labs to healthcare, education, and the arts. More recently, immigrants from Eastern Europe, North Africa, and Central and South America are settling into the area in search of refuge from political turmoil and natural disaster, as well as to procure better living conditions for their families. Immigrant communities that were once primarily European are now Puerto Rican, Asian, and Syrian, with Lehigh County among the top 1 percent of United States counties for immigration.[18]

In 2020, the Lehigh Valley voted 47.8 percent Republican and 52.2 percent Democratic, together representing 5 percent of Pennsylvania's 6,915,283 voters. One of the valley's two counties flipped from majority-Republican to majority-Democratic in the recent elections, making the Lehigh Valley an example of the political diversity and tension that exists across the United States.

This is the environment in which Co.lab.inq sought to listen and learn from religious nones and dones from emerging generations. Your social landscape may be radically different from the Lehigh Valley's. A certain amount of contrast is to be expected; however, the trends that shape our society are likely to be similar and can unite us. Let this, then, serve as both a word of caution and an invitation: This book might not equate to your context, but it will supply insights as you encounter your own rapidly changing community. We offer this as one group's guide to discovering the beauty and the wisdom of others' perspectives and an opportunity to share stories of personal inspiration, belonging, values, adversity, legacy, and assumed beliefs and practices. We invite you to engage with nones and dones in your community who ask: *Hear Us Out.*

F. Qualifiers and Disclaimers

While we have attempted to be rigorous in our approach, following best practices of ethnographic research,[19] we want to be clear about some limitations on our work. The first relates to our sample population for the interviews, in that nones and dones do not make up a clearly defined group. This means that our initial conversation partners self-selected through our social networks. We then asked interviewees to recommend others who were not like themselves and might be willing to participate in our process so that we would have a robust and diverse sample. This broadened our geographic circle to include people from beyond the Lehigh Valley. Thus, we solicited a rolling sample. While we wish we had attracted more ethnic, socioeconomic, and educational diversity among our interviewees, we were able to give a strong voice to those in the LGBTQIA+ population who are often underrepresented. For more detail, see Appendix 2 for a demographic breakdown of our conversation partners.

Second, we had intended to conduct the interviews in person, gathering with small groups of participants. However, the pandemic hit just as we were about to begin the live interview process and all our interviews shifted to Zoom, mostly one-on-one, with a few conducted virtually in groups of two to five respondents. Zoom made transcription much easier and interviews much more consistent. We did not set out to replicate the exemplary studies done by such researchers as Ryan Burge, Melinda Lundquist Denton, Richard Flory, and their colleagues, or the Barna Group. We were interested in pursuing depth rather than scope, and we spent considerable time listening to the varied life experiences of over 200 interviewees.

Third, in formulating our approach to the interviews, we wanted to avoid leading questions that were religious in nature. We devised the following list, which we felt would be clear in providing direction while remaining open-ended and neutral enough to elicit thoughtful and candid responses. If a particular question stumped a respondent, we supplied a follow-up to help clarify their thinking.

1. Tell me a story that has shaped who you are today.

   Follow-up: Who is an important person in your life and how did they help shape who you are today?

2. Tell me about a place/community where you feel you belong.

   Follow-up: Tell me about a place/community where you feel you can be yourself.

3. Tell me about your favorite story, novel, video game, film, or song.

   Follow-up: What is the MIT (most important thing) for you in that story, novel, film, or song?

4. Tell me about a missed opportunity or challenge that has helped to shape who you are today.

   Follow-up: From where or whom do you draw strength or advice when you face a challenge like this?

5. How would you like to be remembered?

   Follow-up: What do you want your legacy to be?

After approximately 10 interviews, the respondents surprised us by inquiring, "Why aren't you asking about our own approach to faith and how it has changed over the years?" We explained that we did not want to make this process "churchy" in any way, but conversation partners responded in no uncertain terms that this question was important to them. They wanted us to pursue it. So, we added a question! Not a single person was reticent about letting us know where they stood on it.

6. If you are a person who has practiced a particular faith tradition, how has your practice changed over the years, if at all? Do you still hold the same faith understanding that you did in your family of origin?

We also asked a bonus question: *Is there anything else you would like to tell us?* We wanted to be sure to allow our conversation partners the ability to share any additional thoughts. We folded poignant responses into our chapters because the themes were wide and varied.

Our primary aim is not to do a religious (or *areligious*) profile of emerging generations, but to begin engaging both people of faith and those who follow no specific religious tradition in what we hope will be an ongoing—indeed, never-ending— discussion. Each chapter will begin with a few quotes inviting you into the creative space we were privileged to enter. Next, you will see a collection of stories offered by both members of Co.lab. inq and our interviewees that sets the stage for the ongoing conversation pertinent to each interview question. Then, you'll encounter our engagement with the print material, conversation transcripts, and personal experiences, inviting you to join the dialogue and discover the rich wisdom collected along the way. Finally, each chapter includes a series of questions for group discussion, extending the conversation into your own context and community.

As you will see, we have endeavored to let our conversation partners speak in their own, unfiltered, voices. And while we have edited them to the extent of selecting quotations from what turned out to be a large body of transcripts, we believe that what we have included is broadly representative of their collective voices. While we have tried to maintain the original wording and raw expression from our oral interviews, some of our conversation partners' reflections have been edited for clarity and grammar. In these places, interviewees were attempting to formulate thoughts and express convictions they had not yet explored out loud. We have made every attempt to capture their honest reflections while also clearly representing them here. This interview process has been for us a qualitative, ethnographic pursuit of understanding, not a data-driven, quantitative research analysis.

Story is the medium of qualitative inquiry, so what you will hear primarily throughout the remainder of this book are the stories of our conversation partners sharing space with Co.lab.inq members.[20] Why stories? To quote Laura Holloway, founder and chief of The Storyteller Agency: "Storytelling offers the opportunity to talk with your audience, not at them." And, as Jimmy Neil Smith, director of the International Storytelling Center, once said: "We are all storytellers. We all live in a network of stories. There isn't a stronger connection between people than storytelling."[21] While each respondent's story was unique, emergent themes rising from our discussions informed and continue to shape our work together.

That said, don't look for definitive conclusions here. There aren't any, and probably never will be. For people of faith, this may be a challenge, a bridge too far. We hope not; hang in there! But the fact is that for the people with whom we spoke, meaning is not fixed. It is a creative, dynamic, relational, and embodied process.

> **Meaning is not fixed. It is a creative, dynamic, relational, and embodied process.**

So... what you have before you is not so much a finished "work" as it is an invitation to join an ongoing conversation. In that spirit, while it is certainly possible to read this in a cozy corner by yourself, we strongly urge you to find a group of folks who would like to engage in this exploration with you. We hope that this will not be one more book to take off your shelf and read in idle moments, but a guide through which to engage with others, to argue, to explore where you concur or disagree with our findings, and to use as a springboard to your own unique conversation. As we learn in the video game *The Legend of Zelda*, it's dangerous to go alone—so don't. Take this guide, and brave companions to travel with you along the way. We are inviting a diverse group of pilgrims to join us, and there may be references and material that will be new to you. Explore them. If you are interested in joining us on this pilgrimage, here is the gear you'll want to bring along:

- An inquisitive mind

- A curious heart

- An attentive ear

- An eye for wisdom and truth

- A disposition of caring

Remember: We are all crossing a bridge that we are in the process of building. We are developing language we do not yet possess. We are all experiencing the conversation together. So...

THE STORIES OF OUR LIVES

James Stahl & Bonnie Bates, Authors
Stephen Simmons, Editor

"The story that shaped who I am today is, very simply, relationships."

—Karen*

"Nothing ever becomes real till it is experienced."

—John Keats

"Nurture your mind with great thoughts. To believe in the heroic makes heroes."

—Benjamin Disraeli

"What we achieve inwardly will change outer reality."

—Plutarch

"Over the years I've had many mentors and people who kind of shaped where I am with my career, personal life, and all that. The person who contributed most of that stuff would be Grandmother—just her morals, values, wisdom, passing on things that she would teach us over the years and spending time with her, seeing how her life was. Seeing her in a committed relationship for years, and obviously her faith in the Lord as well. Learning, being around her, spending time with her, and her example of life, and how to live and love life and enjoy time with her family has been a huge example on how I want to live my life."

—Liz*

Our interviews began by inviting our conversation partners to tell us about a story or experience that shaped them. As humans living in societies, we are shaped and influenced by many things, from experiences that are seen through different lenses, some having to do with culture, language, religion, and family. How we express those stories and experiences also reveals our values and what it is we want to communicate to others as important to us. As *Taylor** realized, "Life is complicated, jobs are, people are... it is OK to be complicated."

JIM'S STORY

I have the opportunity to hear stories from all over the world. My work involves helping people expand their rich storytelling traditions to include hearing and telling biblical stories. We have developed an innovative storytelling process that involves wrestling with Bible stories to discover the original authors' intent and retelling them using their own storytelling language, styles, traditions, and techniques. It never fails that this discovery process helps people find the relevance of Bible stories to their own stories.

When I first entered the biblical storytelling world, I had the privilege to hear Walter Wangerin Jr. as a conference speaker. I still remember some of his stories even 15 years later. One statement I refer to frequently was Wangerin's assertion that we encounter God when our stories connect with God's story. In Matthew T. Dickerson and David L. O'Hara's book, *From Homer to Harry Potter*, Wangerin is quoted as saying, "When one [sic] gazes upon that myth suddenly, in dreadful recognition, cries out, 'There I am! That is me!' then the marvelous translation has occurred: He is lifted out of himself to see himself wholly."[1] I find that the stories people tell are powerful, and they draw us in. When I listen to others tell their stories, it helps me connect to people, their values, traditions, culture, and community.

A. Life Stories

People often think the Bible is irrelevant to their lives. Biblical storytelling audiences around the world often remark after hearing a Bible story *performed* that the story came *alive* to them. Biblical storytellers often reply, "The stories are alive, we just try not to kill them." In telling a biblical story, a person pays attention to intonation, voice, pacing, gestures, expressions, emotions, and presentation; it becomes a part of the storyteller as they interact with the listeners.

Often someone in the audience watching a storytelling performance will say, "I was in that story" or, like a South Sudanese group exclaimed after hearing the story of Jonah, "That's our story! We'd jump ship too if God told us to offer repentance and forgiveness to our enemies." Even though there is much humor and irony in the story of Jonah, there is also a message. Stories draw us in to connect with characters despite being from different cultures and times. "Our lives are entangled in the lives of others and so are our stories. As Paul Ricœur writes, 'The life history of each of us is caught up in the histories of others.'"[2]

Humans are a storytelling species. Jonathan Gottschall reminds us, "A society is composed of fractious people with different personalities, goals, and agendas. What connects us beyond our kinship ties? Story." We tell stories that reveal our beliefs, values, dreams, and life situations. Personal stories are told and formed by life situations and social parameters; they are shaped by the dominant story in that society.

Our conversation partners shared their stories of who they are and what shaped them. We felt privileged to hear their responses and to share with you what we learned. When people tell their stories, the listener hears the storytellers' values, identities, challenges, and how they make sense of the world and their place in it.[3]

Many of our conversation partners shared stories about relationships, the connections they had to their family stories and their relatives, especially their grandparents. They told the stories of their families and how they were shaped by them. Several of the conversation partners noted their grandparents as their role models:

> My grandmother was insanely intelligent, humble, and giving. She was supposedly in the CIA, didn't marry my grandfather until after she had paid off her student loans, and was the first woman in town to open her own bank account to save for college—real poor the whole time.
>
> —*Sophia**

> My grandma and grandpa. He was a minister for 60 years. He did so much not just in the church but for people around him. I remember hearing stories of him in Center City, bringing people in, talking with people in prisons, not forcing religion on them but trying to live a good moral life, be a good person.
>
> —*Octavia**

Others recognized their parents as role models owing to their hard work and the positive values they instilled in their children. At the same time, they acknowledged their parents' limitations and weaknesses, and highlighted opportunities for growth in their own lives. They talked about divorce and estrangement in their families. The conversation partners didn't cast blame, but they understood the challenges.

When I was growing up, my mom was an alcoholic. She still is—that doesn't go away—and she yelled a lot and had a lot of anger issues, and so taught me how *not* to be. Everything that I do, I try not to let my anger get the best of me, and I don't like to yell.

*—Jennifer**

BONNIE'S STORY

In my life there was a history of alcoholism as well: maternal grandfather, mother, two aunts, a first cousin, eventually a brother. As a teen, I became the caregiver, the one who cared for my mother and calmed my father. Yet my memories of childhood are of the strengthening power of love in spite of failings, flaws, and loss. My life became about resiliency and care for others—family and friends, good works in the community, making a difference. That was also an example from my family—even through the hardest days, my parents gave to those less fortunate and taught us to do the same.

B. Grandparent Stories and Biblical Stories

Parents, grandparents, and biblical stories are not items people usually link together. In his book *The Prostitute in the Family Tree*, Douglas Adams states that Bible stories are more like stories grandparents tell their grandchildren. We can identify with grandparent stories as they show hope and characters who are not perfect, while parents' stories tend to be more pointed, cleaned up, idealistic, or indicative of how things or people should be. "If we clean up the biblical stories, we can no longer identify with them; if we share the full story, we can see ourselves in them."[4] In other words, parent stories make you good, while grandparent stories help you understand. Telling a biblical story in the raw, with the rough edges intact, reminds me (Jim) of feedback from telling the story of the first people disobeying God as told in Genesis 3. Teenagers, who heard this story in a church service, approached me two weeks later. They

Parent stories make you good, while grandparent stories help you understand.

were distressed that Adam would be so cruel as to say what he did, blaming God and Eve and not accepting any blame himself. They processed the story and its impact, and heard that Adam was not perfect because the story was not cleaned up.[5]

It is important to note that the storytelling from Genesis 3 resonated in the minds and discussion of the teens mentioned above for two weeks. They were unfamiliar with the Bible, so they asked their friends and searched Google. After finding answers to their questions, they asked the storytellers, who showed them the text in Genesis. The story created dissonance in their minds. *How could Adam be so cruel? Aren't biblical characters supposed to be good?* The students were trying to correct their previous impression that biblical characters were perfect or without blame. They were trying to resolve who they thought Adam was and how he sounded in this story. Arthur Frank, in his book *Letting Stories Breathe*, refers to this interaction as stories being *performative*, not only in being performed by the storyteller, but also in the sense that stories perform in the minds of the storyteller and audience.[6] Stories resonate in the listeners long after the telling, held deep in our memories. This idea of stories being performative is linked to the concept of *interpretive openness*,[7] where we see the story through our experiences and lenses and have "multiple understandings" of it.[8] Although people attempt to train a story or to promote one aspect of it, "Once a story is told, those who have received it have it as theirs and will use it as they will."[9]

Frank rightly follows up this section with the idea that stories are *out of control*, acting on the audience in unanticipated ways.[10] Engaging someone in conversation about the story can be done in a discovery process and not as a prepackaged script with a single intention of telling people what they should get out of the story. Biblical stories are also out of control, and therein lies the beauty of biblical storytelling. These sacred stories are meaningful and intersect with people's lives across time and culture, helping to shape our future. As with the way our conversation partners shared their stories, we frequently forge our own stories out of broken fragments, and at times, learn to forgive and to make peace with difficult events and situations.

> **Biblical stories are also out of control, and therein lies the beauty of biblical storytelling.**

C. Family Stories

Michael W. Pratt and Barbara H. Fiese state in *Family Stories and the Life Course* that "Families are thus stage, company, and audience for us all across the life cycle, and stories are an intimate part of that process."[11] Some of the family stories in our interviews included challenges and adversity. We'll return to this theme in chapter 4. As *Nevaeh**, a conversation partner who lost family, said, "Life is suffering, I believe that if I have a belief system, it is that life is suffering, and we can decide to help each other through that, or not."

Over and over our conversation partners talked about the influence of their families: good and bad situations, and the inspiration and values derived from those relationships. *Lori** didn't realize how tight and close her family was until she went off to college. She said, "When I think back to my earliest memories, I recall being surrounded by a lot of family, and I think that I'm very lucky and fortunate that I grew up with the family that I do have." *Thomas** said,

> When I first volunteered with my father in the fire department, I saw what he did outside our home life, and how much time and effort and other things he sacrificed. He saw things, and at the end of the day he would have to come home with a clear mind and be a strong person. I think a lot of what he saw there—and what trickled down to me essentially—was really positive. I always try to have a good outlook and always be there to help people, to lend a hand and volunteer. I think that really impacted me a lot.

*Noelle** shared,

> The number one thing would be when my mom left the family. I was in fourth grade and she just kind of disappeared. It was just me and my dad, and that really shaped who I am in so many facets of my life: hard work, my attitude, my interests, who I am as a person. Who I am today really developed just from that in itself.

Consistently, the presence and absence of strong familial relationships prove key in shaping the stories we communicate about ourselves, and the story in which we participate alongside others.

D. Experiencing Cultural Diversity

When people share stories of what shapes and influences them, cultural diversity cannot be ignored. As we share stories together, we expand our cultural and linguistic diversity. This occurs in a number of ways, and was clear as we reviewed the interview statements of our conversation partners. Some people expand their cultural diversity by choice. *Stella** describes finding a new friend as a result of being late for the school bus. They did a lot together, including joining a travel club. She says:

> We went to Europe in high school. It was eye-opening and life-changing for me—I got real interested in travel, in the world, and I ultimately majored in international relations and geography in college. It led me to travel and see other parts of the world, and it led her to do the same. She's lived in India and Nepal, and it's all from being late for the bus that day.

Not only are people traveling to other places around the world to experience other cultures, but regions like the Lehigh Valley are diversifying with new cultural groups. In this way, others can experience an expansive cultural diversity by exposure or contact. At one time in this area, the dialect of Pennsylvania German (known locally as Pennsylvania Dutch) was a language of wider communication. Residents with no German ethnicity learned to speak it to trade and communicate with ethnic Pennsylvania Germans. Language patterns changed drastically during the world wars. Many people spoke Pennsylvania German as their first language and in the home. When they attended elementary school in the 1930s, however, they were punished for speaking anything but English. At one time, Bethlehem had people from many parts of Europe who brought their cultures and languages. These immigrants started their own churches, some of which are still gathering, such as the Greek, Ukrainian, Russian, and Syrian Orthodox churches.

So, change in language-use trends affects us all. As population groups continue to change, cultural diversity shifts with it, and people adapt to varying degrees alongside the large cultural shifts we encounter. For example, currently both the mayor of Allentown and the police chief speak Spanish fluently, and Spanish is now close to being a majority language in Allentown. There are several churches in the Lehigh Valley where Spanish is the language used in the worship service. Also, there are four Spanish-language newspapers in circulation in this area. The Lehigh Valley is also home to a large Arabic-speaking population. One of our regular grocery stores is staffed by Arabic speakers. While shopping for groceries in the valley, one can also hear various other non-European languages, including Amharic, Hindi and Urdu, Malayali, Mandarin, Turkish, Farsi and Dari, Pashto, Hebrew, Burmese, and Jamaican.

Finally, in our rapidly changing world there are numerous opportunities available to expand and exchange stories of cultural diversity. Travel and the internet make our world accessible and allow us to see how other people think, communicate, and tell the stories that shape their lives and world. A person living in the Lehigh Valley can learn about the Moravians, attend the Celtic Classic Festival, and also hear live performances of Native American stories and the Ramayana. They can sample non-European cuisines from around the world, like Jamaican jerk chicken and goat curry, Thai, Burmese, Korean, Chinese, Japanese, and North and South Indian foods.

Travel and the internet make our world accessible and allow us to see how other people think, communicate, and tell the stories that shape their lives and world.

Cross-cultural experiences help people gain awareness of other ways of living and highlight customs and values of our own cultures in ways that can foster reflection and evaluation. It is not surprising that generations with more exposure to other people groups have developed a greater degree of tolerance and appreciation toward people from other cultures. Several conversation partners expressed lessons they learned about trying to understand other points of view and respecting all people.

E. Life Is a Journey

The concept or value that life is a journey was a common metaphor articulated by our conversation partners. Being able to tell one's journey as a story is an important aspect of life and our well-being. People often think that journey stories should conform to scripts that have either been passed on to them through family or dictated by the greater society, regardless of whether these stories have to do with family, career choices, spirituality, physical health, or mental health. The people represented in our conversations narrated their stories with a certain amount of fluidity, contingency, and change. As they reflected on turning points in their lives, they were able to see the need for change in direction and conviction while maintaining a strong sense of self.

Emery*, another of our conversation partners, shared about the difficulties of moving from Puerto Rico and finding that he and his family were not always welcomed, apart from their Puerto Rican community. "Puerto Ricans are a tight-knit community and more have moved to the area from the island, so we made that connection. That's our main community and it definitely made it a lot easier, but it took a couple of years for that to happen."

Stories of resiliency like Emery's will be highlighted in other chapters of this book, but clearly family stories and experiences deeply influenced our conversation partners. They are looking for honesty in connections—real connections that acknowledge the strengths and weaknesses of the people with whom they are in relationship.

F. People, Brands, and Taking Stands

This search for genuine relationships extends to the marketplace, religious communities, and other organizations. For instance, surveys show that before emerging generations purchase products, they research the social positions taken by the producer. How do organizations respond to issues like LGBTQIA+ and abortion rights when some states are limiting their scope? What happens to a brand that continues to do business with Russia, which is committing genocide and war crimes in Ukraine? If an organization does nothing to create gender equity, overlooks the poor, neglects the homeless, and does not extend a helping hand to single mothers, what then? What story does a brand's marketing tell about their convictions, values, and the people impacted by corporate policy and practice? These issues matter to our conversation partners.

Mike Proulx states that Gen Z will drop a brand more quickly than people from previous generations if the brand's social stance does not fit theirs.[12] They do not trust what's being pushed on them. Proulx warns, "To reach Gen Z requires that marketers embrace the interconnectedness of profit and purpose. While many brands are now jumping on the "purpose-led" bandwagon, most aren't seen as conscious companies that pass Gen Z's sniff test."[13]

For example, one of our conversation partners, *Vivian**, recalled growing up in a rural area that fell victim to chemical pollution from a major company. In response, she changed her career path from engineering to environmental science. As Tyler Huckabee notes:

> And they [Gen Z] expect the same from institutions they're a part of and the brands they follow. In the past, for-profit companies and institutions like churches could

skate by without taking a stand on social issues, but two out of three members of Gen Z expect companies to have a position on social issues and 72 percent say brands need to care about things like the environment, humanitarian causes, and social issues.[14]

There was very little comment on institutions or workplaces with our conversation partners. There was not a lot of "name-brand" focus. Rather, they look for high quality, usefulness, and reasonable pricing. Telling the story of a brand is less important than the relationships that can be built with local business and hearing the stories of those businesses as community mem-

It's not about the institutions, but the people, their stories, and their relationships.

bers. It's not about the institutions, but the people, their stories, and their relationships. Emerging generations recognize that taking a stand for the benefit of communities is crucial to the story that will shape successive generations. It is the work of each generation to discover how sacred stories connect with contemporary lives to inspire expressions of God's commands to love God and to love one another, to protect and cherish the world, and to work for social justice.

G. Why Is the Church Losing Them?

This is where the church is running into trouble with Gen Z. Nine out of ten Americans say the American church is "too judgmental." Nearly as many say it's hypocritical. Seventy percent of Americans say the church is "insensitive to others," and one-third say the American church is characterized by "moral failures in leadership."[15] Ow!

Our conversation partners shared stories that aren't always rosy and filled with joy, but they are unabashedly honest about the challenges in their lives. They seek to be in relationship with others who can be as honest. The church has often failed to be honest about its flaws, to live into its values, and to follow in the footsteps of the scriptural storytellers.

The church has often failed to be honest about its flaws, to live into its values, and to follow in the footsteps of the scriptural storytellers.

and to follow in the footsteps of the scriptural storytellers. Biblical stories are not cleaned up. They are messy.

In 2018, a Cigna study found that Gen Z is easily the loneliest generation of Americans: 46 percent of Americans feel lonely some of the time, but that number climbs up to 69 percent with Gen Z. Moreover, 68 percent of Gen Z feel like nobody knows them well.[16] That lack of connection can't be met by a brand, a corporation, or an institution. But it can be met by people who reach out to them with empathy, love, and understanding. If the church starts empowering the members of Gen Z in their own pews to build relationships with their peers, they'll not only be building relationships with America's loneliest generation, but also be proving that American Christians are truly interested in the people outside their buildings on Sunday mornings.[17]

For example, *Eliana** shared the story of being confronted by her Christian friends who identified as LGBTQIA+. Her church background had led her to believe that such friends were not Christian, and that exploring such issues is dangerous. These friends helped *Eliana** explore that "dangerous" territory and invited her to ask questions previously considered out-of-bounds. She attended one church where the pastor commended her on her "faith journey,... a really healthy road to go down." Even though she no longer identifies as Christian herself, she continues to attend that church and participate. She stated, "I learned a lot. About me, people, grace in the whole experience."

Conversation partners who had stories in which the church proved welcoming often had exemplary family members who lived out their faith. *Ruby** was positively influenced by the church and her family. She says:

> I was born into families that really value family and are fairly religious, but incredibly loving. Seeing their passion for helping others, being surrounded by that loving and care for others, and the desire to bring about positive change in the world is something that has really shaped who I am.

Grace* also had a positive church experience, where she was welcomed by a different family in that church. She said about her life-changing experience:

> I would say I grew up with an unhealthy family. When I came to my current church, I met a family who completely welcomed me into their home. It was like they adopted me—not a second family, but they have been my family for 15-plus years. That completely reshaped how I thought about my traditional family. It affects the way I have relationships with other people and welcome others into my life. It really changed me.

H. Expectations

This chapter represents the first part of the interview, and the interviewers noticed that the conversation partners were somewhat hesitant and surprised by our approach. This could be attributed to typical behavior at the beginning of an interview process. It could also be that the conversation partners were expecting questions about the church, such as if, when, and where they attended church, and if not, why not? Possibly they expected the equivalent of parent stories and got grandparent stories instead. In other words, they may have been expecting a survey with limited scope or multiple-choice questions and very brief input, rather than interviewers who listened to their stories.

I. Summary

We have explored our conversation partners' stories and found their inspiration to have come from experiences with relationships. Their stories, representing both positive and negative situations, were often about family relationships. Ideally, these stories will inspire them to move forward in their lives. Their accounts were honest and open, and often demonstrated empathy and personal growth.

On a related note, organizations that demonstrate a sense of integrity, welcomeness, diversity, compassion, and empathy in our society are likely to attract Gen Y and Gen Z people. Our population is continuing to diversify and will most likely continue to trend that way. The world is close by, and young people are venturing out to explore the world and not living insularly.

We have also explored the dynamics of biblical stories and their connection to our daily lives. In those ancient sacred stories, we can look into the stories and see ourselves, connecting themes, motifs, various life situations, and our stories. Bible stories, when told in full and not as piecemeal snippets, allow us to see the biblical characters on their spiritual journeys, delve into their emotions, connect and identify with them, and learn what God was doing in their lives.

The same can be said of people when we allow others to tell their stories in full and accompany them on the journey of inspirational discovery performed in mutual, relational storytelling. We encourage our readers to expand your experience of cultural diversity by engaging the full, rich heritage of other cultures, which can enrich your own story.

J. For Further Group Discussion

1. Gather in small groups and tell a story that shaped who you are today. Be honest and real in the conversation. This may require some trust building, but sharing stories is key to building strong relationships. What did you learn from your story? From others' stories?

2. What life stories resonated with your group? Discuss commonalities and differences.

3. What are the stories told in your family of origin, and how did they impact you? How do your family relationships affect the stories you tell?

4. Connect personal stories with the stories of others. Connect the stories generationally. Connect the stories with sacred stories, but don't limit this to Christian scripture. Explore what the participants know of stories from ecumenical and interfaith relationships.

LONGING FOR BELONGING

Sue Pizor Yoder & Jill Peters, Authors
James Stahl, Editor

"Why am I afraid to tell you who I am? I am afraid to tell you who I am, because, if I tell you who I am, you may not like who I am, and it's all that I have..."

—John Joseph Powell

"It isn't much good having anything exciting, if you can't share it with somebody."

—Winnie the Pooh

"I've always felt a longing for belonging..."

—*Sally**

SUE'S STORY

I grew up feeling very loved. I was the greatly anticipated and desired first girl child on both sides of my family. I was surrounded by kids in my ever-expanding suburban neighborhood with whom I had many adventures exploring life together. At age five, my younger brother was born with Down syndrome. For my mother, David very much belonged in our family. For my father, David didn't, and should have been institutionalized. In retrospect, I think my five-year-old little self struggled to understand this clash of perspective. Did he belong or didn't he? I had grown up in the church and so I took seriously the earliest song I learned: "Jesus loves me, this I know, for the Bible tells me so."[1] I figured if God loved red and yellow, black, and white, that meant God loved people like David too. I concluded he belonged, and I loved him fiercely and would take on anyone who sent any message to the contrary.

As I grew up, I became very active in school and other activities. I had a lot of places where I felt I fit in, as an officer in student government, in musicals and select ensembles, in a fraternal organization where I was very active, and in supporting many of my brother's friends who had a variety of disabilities. In most ways, life was relatively carefree for me: my basic needs were met, I had a supportive family, I enjoyed school, I had a wide variety of friends, I was part of a church that guided me in good decision-making, and I had safe places and people if needed. That helped me grow through adolescence and into young adulthood.

By college, I realized that my dad was an alcoholic. I was late to fully acknowledge this because unlike many alcoholics, my dad became more loving and kinder when drinking, so alcohol didn't seem like a liability. Identifying his addiction helped me identify my tendencies toward codependency and living out my life as the "hero" child in my family system. I whipped through college in three-and-a-half years and began teaching second grade. Having felt called and then re-called to become a pastor, I soon enrolled in seminary. While there, I met my husband, Bob, who was completing dental school. We fell deeply in love and were married the summer before our respective senior years.

While I knew Bob loved me very deeply and that we belonged together, his parents objected. They did not think he should marry a professional woman, or one who had a mind of her own, or one who might produce a child with Down syndrome. They made it clear that I didn't belong. This was utterly disorienting to me. I had always felt like I belonged wherever I was. This experience sent me on a quest to understand the significance of belonging in new ways.

A. The Quest for Belonging

What does it mean to *belong* in our increasingly divisive and disconnected world? "Belonging" is a primal need of all human beings. We need to belong to ourselves as much as we need to belong to others. Think of all that people do and say to "fit in." We hustle for acceptance and approval. We are wired in our DNA with a need to belong! People are programmed to want connection and belonging, but not by giving away their sense of self, freedom, status, or power. Let's take a glance at what we know about *belonging*.

In 1943, psychology professor Abraham Maslow wrote about the hierarchy of human needs. Since then, others have visualized his concepts into a pyramid of five levels with our most basic needs, the physiological, at the bottom: air, food, water, shelter, clothing, and sleep. Maslow next identified the human need for safety and security, including health, family, and stability. In the middle of the hierarchy, he recognized the important human need for love and belonging, which focuses on our craving for friendship, family, intimacy, and connection. Maslow developed this system while living with and studying the Siksika (Blackfoot) Confederacy of Tribes in the US.[2] After taking care of the communal needs of the first level, and the safety and security needs of family, health and stability, Siksika tribal communities offered the deep connections of family, intimacy, friendship, and belonging.

Here we discovered a real link to our conversation partners. Desiring to explore how they fulfill this basic human need for belonging, we asked: **"Tell us about a place or community where you feel that you belong."** We were fascinated to note that in answering this question, many of our conversation partners talked about their "tribe" and its importance in their lives. In the book *Tribe*, Sebastian Junger explored tribal societies, which embody loyalty, belonging, and the age-old human quest for meaning. He did extensive research on the Indigenous, tribal societies of North America during the time before the American Revolution. European transplants were attracted to these groups. Many integrated into them *and left their own cultures behind* because of the strong and compelling sense of belonging.[3]

Junger also traced similar stories through many different North American tribes. Further, he documented stories of deep belonging in bombed out London during World War II, in the displaced people of New Orleans during hurricane Katrina, in his own journalistic experiences in war-torn Serbia, after an earthquake in 1915 Italy, after civil wars in Spain, Algeria, Lebanon, and Northern Ireland, and in the stories of soldiers with post-traumatic stress disorder (PTSD). *The common thread is that during a crisis or war, peoples' mental health is seemingly better than it is later, when they are out of the crisis.*[4] The sense of belonging is so great that people not only survive but *thrive* in difficult situations. It is afterward, when they are disconnected from a community of purpose, that people flounder. In the case of PTSD, a majority of vets who experience this have *not* seen combat.[5] In the early air campaigns of the first Gulf War, 80 percent of the psychiatric US casualties came from support units that took almost no incoming fire.[6] Like freed prisoners who are suddenly disconnected from their incarcerated "tribe," some people find it very difficult to function in normal situations where they have no connections, no sense of tribe.

The downside of belonging to a tribe is the temptation not to allow others entry and to make the group boundaries as if they were posted with "do not enter" signs. There is a distinction between belonging to a tribe and the movement toward tribalism. Here the group is often fueled by a dysfunctional competition and loyalty to the tribe that promotes anxiety, fear, and prejudice instead of courage, support, and confidence. In this scenario, a person must hustle for approval and acceptance by the tribe. We see this today, for example, in street gangs and political parties. But these requirements are the greatest *barriers* to belonging. Belonging to a group may require us to get uncomfortable, to be vulnerable, to learn how to be with people without sacrificing who we are. As we are currently experiencing, the negative effects of tribalism make us more susceptible to fake news, propaganda, and conflict. At the same time, humans still need to belong to their tribes.

The majority of people living in the US have descended from immigrants and have historically found identity and belonging amid faith communities. The church or synagogue served not only as a worship space, but often as a school and social center for immigrant groups. Allentown, Bethlehem, and Easton, Pennsylvania, are representative of many developing towns during the Industrial Revolution in the United States. New immigrants moved to the Lehigh Valley, often encouraged by their own people who had already transitioned and by ethnic church leaders who were given incentives by Bethlehem Steel to recruit new workers. Waves of immigrants were also independently attracted to these cities for the relatively lucrative jobs available for unskilled workers. The opportunity was there to apprentice and advance, procuring what they thought was a secure future for their children and their children's children. Germans, Italians, Polish, Portuguese, Windish, and later Puerto Rican families relocated to the Lehigh Valley. By the time the Puerto Rican families arrived, however, industry was waning, leaving those immigrants with only the *promise* of a better financial future that was void in reality.

As each group arrived, they settled into a neighborhood with a Protestant and/or Catholic Church as their anchors. Grocery stores, bakeries, and eventually restaurants followed.

Neighborhoods were a place of identity. Kids played together, people walked to church, adults hung out in the evenings and talked, and you borrowed sugar from your neighbor to save a trip to the store. These communities offered to one another the comfort of *being known.* They enjoyed similar foods, spoke in their mother tongues, shared music and recreational pastimes, and practiced familiar traditions. They helped people feel like they belonged in a new and wholly foreign environment. These enclaves of culture helped each group build connections, a sense of belonging, and eventual stability. In Bethlehem's Southside where Bethlehem Steel was located, many immigrant workers lived in ethnic neighborhoods. As generations learned English, advanced through the working ranks, and became more educated, they slowly moved away from the proximity of the mills to other parts of Bethlehem and the Lehigh Valley.[7] Wealthier families soon formed exclusive recreational clubs. Different ethnic groups worked, worshipped, and played separately. The explosion of the suburbs after World War II further scattered old urban neighborhoods. The ethnic ties stretched as people lived in more integrated neighborhoods, joined other churches, and intermarried. Although ethnic pride was still present, the new common bonds of English, shared foods, and mixed neighborhoods shifted those initial strong bonds.

Our first-generation conversation partners reported a similar experience, with strong ethnic ties to family, food, faith, and language. It is noteworthy that many of our second-generation partners also reported strong ethnic ties. As *Tierra** shared, "I would say my belonging is in the African community. It's a place I belong because we speak the same language, and I feel like I can have a piece of home." Or as *Regina** shared:

> I grew up in an Italian family, so I have hundreds of cousins and aunts and uncles, and no matter how distant,

whether someone is like a sixth cousin once removed, they're basically like my brother or sister and being around all of them always makes me feel like I belong with everyone. It was just amazing growing up in my family. We're all still close and we're near each other and that's really important to me.

While many found belonging in their ethnic groups, the number one answer given to our question about belonging was clearly "family," named by over 20 percent of respondents. But what does family mean?

JILL'S STORY

In my family of origin, when we got together for holidays, we were all related by blood or marriage. It was the same group every year. Nothing changed. The menu was fixed, the location was always the same, and, although older, the people were all the same, sometimes even wearing the same holiday clothes from year to year! Fast-forward to my house decades later. There are 24 people gathered for the holidays and I'm only related to one—my mom—by blood, and related to one by marriage, my husband. My stepson and his wife and kids are there, my three adopted kids, who are siblings, are there with their significant others. My grandchildren, some of whom are half-siblings, are all running around, laughing. One of my grandsons was adopted out around age three, so his adoptive family joins us. This is my new family. Not together by blood, but by design and thought and intentionality.

B. A New Definition of Family

Just as neighborhoods have changed, we discovered that families have changed a great deal over the last several decades. In fact, the mid-twentieth-century stereotype of the white American family—mom and dad, two-point-five kids, and a dog—had already made a dramatic shift by the 1970s. Cultural changes included an increased divorce rate, women in the workplace, greater access to birth control, changing family structures, soldiers returning from Vietnam, and an ongoing sexual revolution. Two decades later, this shift was unambiguously named by Barney, the purple dinosaur. One of the songs from this children's show is "My Family's Just Right for Me." Each verse describes a different family construct as a part of the refrain affirms, *A family is people, and a family is love. That's a family.* The refrain ends by welcoming diversity: *They come in different sizes and different kinds, But mine's just right for me.* When the purple dinosaur sang this song, he declared and welcomed a shift in how the concept of family was viewed. Notice there is no mention of family bonds based on bloodline. Families now come in many different shapes with a key ingredient being love. According to Barney, it does not matter what yours looks like.

C. Pathways to Belonging

For Jews and Christians, consider that our traditions' opening story is one that identifies our need to belong. Given the creative opportunity to name and relate to all the animals of creation by the Creator, the "one created of red earth" or "earthling" (*adam* in Hebrew) is not content. While there is great diversity, there is no one of the earth creature's tribe. The Creator recognizes the creature's need to belong in community (Genesis 2:18). The creature craves to belong in community (Genesis 2:20), and the creature is delighted when the Creator offers another one made of the red earth, one like itself, yet different (*adama* in Hebrew). We consequently learn *throughout* the ancient narrative that the Creator desires *relationship* with this created community.

This theme is enhanced in the Christian New Testament, where a special kind of relationship in community, *koinonia*, is offered both with and between the Creator and the created. Koinonia is an intimate spiritual com-

Koinonia is defined as an intimate spiritual communion and participative sharing with each other and with their Creator.

munion and participative sharing with each other and with their Creator. In the words of the late Rev. Keith Brown:

> Koinonia is a community of two or more persons who are seeking to practice the Christ-like love that will create a safe place in which to share one's joys and sorrows, victories and defeats, doubts and convictions, fears and hopes, and temptations and sins, without experiencing condemnation, rejection, too much advice, or a breach of confidence.[8]

When embodied, koinonia generates an atmosphere of unconditional love where one can be their authentic self (good, bad, and ugly) without fear of rejection. Jesuit Priest John Powell wrote about the reason people shy away from this koinonia gift that is offered: "Why am I afraid to tell you who I am? I am afraid to tell you who I am, because, if I tell you who I am, you may not like who I am, and it's all that I have."[9]

Many recent studies show that locating a sense of belonging in close social relationships and with our community is essential to well-being. We need, and are created for, one another to survive. As Brené Brown discovered in her research on belonging, we cannot know true belonging until we have the courage to share our most authentic selves with people. Our sense of belonging can never be greater than our level of self-acceptance.[10]

Our conversation partners shared with us the value and importance of a community that creates a safe place to share who we *really* are. Imagine an environment where we can share the good, the bad, and the ugly and find ourselves loved *despite* what we reveal. Perhaps if the church were more like an Alcoholics Anonymous (AA) meeting, its doors would be swinging wide open with eager partakers. Recovery groups offer an environment where participants practice koinonia by owning their reality/addiction while recovering from its devastating path amid a community of support and encouragement. If there is one thing our research repeatedly revealed, it was the desire and need for authentic, accepting, honest community.

D. Barriers to Belonging

Pastor Grant Skeldon reports that millennials who no longer attend church perceive Christians as:[11]

- Judgmental (87%)

- Hypocritical (85%)

- Anti-homosexual (91%)

- Insensitive to others (70%)

Ouch! We have to stop *talking about* emerging generations and start *listening to* them. If you are among those we interviewed or a none or done reading this book, thank you for speaking your truth to us.

We have to stop *talking about* emerging generations and start *listening to* them.

We tend to want emerging generations to come to us and continue to pass on the torch of the faith that we have found meaningful. However, as Lia

McIntosh, Jasmine Rose Smothers, and Rodney Thomas Smothers suggest in *Blank Slate: Write Your Own Rules for a 22nd Century Church Movement,* "Everyone is depending on us to save an institution that we're not connected to and clean up a mess that we didn't create."[12] Imagine if emerging adults, who may be looking for a place to belong, discovered faith communities that advocate for:

- The voiceless poor and homeless
- Efforts toward reconciliation instead of retribution
- The care of creation
- Peacemaking efforts

STEVE'S STORY

I believe that my grandparents would have found the question of "belonging" completely mystifying. My grandparents belonged to the Methodist Church, the Republican party, the white (and, in their experience, pretty much the only) race, a number of civic and fraternal organizations, and, more broadly, a small rural community in Illinois. To a great extent, these categories constituted their identity and where they believed they belonged; they didn't have to worry about constructing it themselves. I don't think it would have ever occurred to them to agonize about where they belonged.

E. Social Networks

Our conversation partners responded quite differently than Steve's grandparents. Few mentioned any of these kinds of belonging. This may indicate the collapse of "social capital" in contemporary US society that Robert D. Putnam described in his influential book *Bowling Alone: The Collapse and Revival of American Community.*

Putnam explored the difference between "bonding social networks" that are inward-looking and "bridging social networks" which are outward-looking and include people across "diverse social cleavages." Social capital has eroded steadily, and sometimes dramatically, over the past two generations.[13] Putnam traced decreases in seven separate measures of social capital in the United States (political, civic, and religious participation; workplace and informal networks; mutual trust; and altruism) right up to the present. His findings indicated four key reasons: pressures of time and money, mobility and sprawl, television, and generational differences. While TV was the number one contributor in Putnam's study recorded in 2000, the cellphone has clearly surpassed these percentages, with millennials spending 21.7 hours per week on their smartphones in 2015. Their laptops and readers serve more like bodily extensions than learning aids.[14] Another 2015 study shows Gen Z spends even more time on their phones, with high school seniors spending six hours on their iPhone a day *just during their leisure time*. To quote one teenager: "I know I shouldn't, but I just can't help it. Having my phone closer to me while I'm sleeping is a comfort."[15]

F. Networks by Origin/Networks by Choice

In our interviews, the top places respondents indicated they experienced belonging included:

- Family: 20%

- Workmates or work: 17%

- Sports teams or yoga or games: 14%

- College or high school friends: 13.5%

- Friends in general 12%

- Arts/music/theater 10%

Overall, our conversation partners shared phrases like I can "be myself," "no judgment," "accept me," "my safe place," "a place for me," "like-minded," "at home" to indicate what constituted a place of belonging. Several respondents indicated that they felt they belonged *any*where. As one respondent indicated, "I know there's a place where I belong, so I just make myself belong everywhere." Or, consider *Dave** who shared, "There isn't anywhere that I feel I don't belong... I feel like I can just be myself everywhere because I am who I am and that's how I present myself."

A few observations: Among all our conversation partners, only two experienced a sense of belonging via a club or organization (Rotary and Girl Scouts specifically). Our interviewees did not experience belonging through civic or fraternal organizations. Declining memberships in service and fraternal organizations, faith communities, and social clubs indicate that emerging generations are not joiners in conventional organizations.

Fewer than 5 percent responded with any sense of belonging through social media. Online communities are frequently based on superficial exchanges instead of meaningful conversation. Given that having more "friends" on social media is a status symbol, it is no surprise that girls and young women in particular are constantly in search of likes and positive comments on their social networks, with persistent pressure to post sexy and revealing photos. And for many teens, belonging or not belonging often feels like life or death. Boys and young men are more often found competitively playing video games. Psychologist Jean Twenge indicated that in 2015, 9 percent of teens said they played more than 40 hours per week (the time commitment of a full-time job).[16] More recently, these gender lines have become more fluid; boys are sharing nudes and girls are playing video games. Smartphones are often perceived as both bane and blessing.

One group to highlight were the 10 percent of respondents who indicated that they don't belong anywhere. Their responses were open and honest: "A sense of belonging is actually something that has eluded me quite a bit in the later years of my 20s," "I literally can't think of anywhere," "Well, I kind of don't," and "I have always felt a longing for belonging." Could this be tied to the largest mental health crisis in decades? Speaking of youth Jane McGonigal writes:

> An "under thirty" group of over ten thousand rising entre-preneurs, scientists, activists, and community leaders from 165 countries was polled by the WEF [World Economic Forum] for their top future forces. Interestingly, this group named *mental health deterioration* just above climate change and economic inequality as their number one future force that will have the biggest global impact over the next decade. While surprising—mental health deterioration has never appeared in a *Global Risk Report* before—it also makes sense. The years 2020 and 2021 marked the largest global increases in depression, anxiety, grief, burnout, loneliness, and trauma ever observed, due to the pandemic and its long-term aftereffects.[17]

Loneliness has increased, and internet bullying is soaring. For the first time, in 2016, the majority of students entering college described their mental health as below average.[18] Suicide rates are higher than ever among emerging generations. These general themes appeared multiple times throughout our research, which suggests many factors contribute to this shift in mental health. For example:

- The rise of incivility and the trend toward seeking popularity by hurting or aggressively bullying another person.

- Diminished capacity to wait. Instant gratification is the norm, yet many things require long-term commitment.

- Challenges finding the work-life balance they desire.

- Feeling more entitled to high compensation, benefits, and career advancement than employers are willing to offer.

- Decreased financial giving, volunteer, and community service that can lead to self-absorption.

- The decline of in-person social interaction.

- Lack of sleep due to interacting with their cell phones 24/7.

- A lack of age-appropriate independence due to helicopter parenting.

G. So What Does All of This Suggest?

What might be some learnings or thoughts to consider in light of our common human need to belong? The Harvard study *Something More* discovered in December 2016 that many religiously unaffiliated millennials found meaning and belonging in makerspaces, coworking hubs, dinner parties, fitness boot camps, and fan communities. While these organizations are secular, they demonstrate elements of religious

In fact, many unaffiliated participants in these communities have not left religion behind; rather they are finding spiritual life outside religious institutions.

polity, liturgy, and even spirituality. This perhaps raises the question of who owns religion? These groups are gesturing toward new ways that "religious life" might be realized in the future. In fact, many unaffiliated participants in these communities have not left religion behind; rather, they are finding spiritual life out-side religious institutions. The authors of this study identified six themes that comprise the cultural DNA of this growing move-ment: community, personal transformation, social transforma-tion, purpose-finding, creativity, accountability... and "something more." There will be more about this in chapters 3 and 6. Stay tuned.

What does materialism say to rising generations? Your value is in your capacity to consume. Imagine if religious institutions were bolder in declaring there is more to life than consumption and possessions. Materialism often leaves us thirsting for more. Imagine the power of a countercultural message. The Harvard study *Something More* discovered that what matters most to young Americans is guiding values and a sense of connection to the nat-ural world and to all that is bigger than ourselves.[19] Two forms of disparate communities are emerging in American society: secular communities that are meaningful and rapidly growing yet strug-gling to engage with life's ultimate questions, and creative, inno-vative religious communities that are drawing from deep wells of wisdom but struggling to attract rising generations. Imagine the possibilities if faith communities and emerging generations listen to one another, explore possibilities together, and invite conver-sations that engage questions such as *What would be life-giving to you at this moment? How might we engage in purposeful work, play, and service together? How would you structure communities of mutual support, encouragement, and creativity? What helps you expe-rience "something more"?*

Columnist David Brooks brings another perspective to our need to belong in his book *The Second Mountain: The Quest for a Moral Life.* Brooks discusses how easily our search for partner, family, setting up home, and starting a career causes us to lose sight of the wider world. While trying to succeed in career and grow into adulthood, our focus is on ourselves, our needs, and desires. Many reach a place in life where they ask the question *Is this all there is in life?* Upon re-evaluating their lifestyle, choices, and career, some find a vocation, a way of giving to the community by contributing to the wider good of society. These people, he suggests, find their "second mountain" and get involved in a cause without heed of renumeration, often sacrificing time, resources, safety, and self. No longer looking for rewards, acknowledgement, or noticeable measures of success, they often find fulfillment, purpose, and belonging.

Individuals and whole societies have always asked questions in search of meaning and purpose: *What is my best life? What do I believe in? Where do I belong?* Many trudge along, too afraid to make a change. Some become paralyzed by self-focus. Our hyper-individualism has led to a society where people live farther and farther apart from each other: socially, politically, emotionally, civically, and physically.[20] This has resulted in a loneliness crisis, suffering, distrust, alienation, lack of meaningful purpose, and polarization for many. And while tribalism appears to be a way out of the loneliness and suffering, the connections are often based on a common foe or mutual hatred as previously suggested.

Brooks proposes a strong need for role models/mentors and connecting with honorable people who have made choices in life that command respect and admiration.[21] Much of our research suggests that emerging generations are very open to such mentoring relationships. Members of Co.lab.inq who have been working with emerging adults have heard similar desires for models and mentors. Young adults are seeking a reciprocal relationship, open to a free flow of wisdom from one generation to the next and back again. Such relationships open the possibility of difficult conversations, where navigating discourse with people with whom we disagree can be learned and respected. Our experience indicates helpful qualities in mentoring relationships include:

- Integrity and faithfulness (keeping one's word and honoring one's commitment to the relationship)

- Availability (willingness to accommodate)

- Teachability (this must be a two-way street with trust established; teaching how to lead with love in our relationships is critical)

- Humility (on both sides so that each can continue to grow and learn)

- Compatibility (some level of chemistry in the relationship)

- The desire to grow (a hunger for learning new tools and frameworks from the other is essential)

- Wisdom (a willingness to mutually share knowledge and expertise)

H. Summary

A sense of belonging is a fundamental human need and desire. Being "part of a group" looks very different today than it did for previous generations.

Emerging generations find a sense of belonging in very different ways than their grandparents or great-grandparents did. While family remains very important, the concept of family has been redefined and now has a much wider scope.

Church connections, while important for some, are also lessening or being reconfigured for younger generations. The challenge for the church, where concepts like membership and attendance are measures of faithfulness, is not only to understand how emerging generations operate but also to not try to change them to fit traditional molds. The fundamental desire to belong is still present with them, but they won't belong on institutional terms.

Since isolation is a growing problem, we can assist each other in collaborating to discover how to create good places to be and grow. We can create communities, makerspaces, and mentoring relationships that offer pathways to belonging.

Emerging generations long for authentic forms of belonging characteristic of koinonia groups. When people feel fully loved and accepted, they can realize their full potential and offer their best self to community.

I. For Further Group Discussion

1. Describe a place or community where you feel like you belong.

2. How has this chapter changed your thoughts or feelings about belonging?

3. Who would be someone outside your social circles you could connect with? How might you connect? How might that be a challenge? How might we share in a spirit of generosity as we engage one another?

4. Name five ways you make connections inside and outside institutions. If you are a member of a faith community, how are you doing in offering opportunities to those outside your walls? If you are not in a faith community and such opportunities were made available through a local faith community, would you be open to participating? Why or why not?

5. The Harvard study identified themes that comprise the cultural DNA of a growing movement among young adults: community, personal transformation, social transformation, purpose-finding, creativity,

accountability, and "something more." Who offers these things in your community? How?

6. We defined koinonia as an intimate spiritual communion and participative sharing with each other and with the Creator. Have you ever experienced this kind of belonging? Where? If not, how might you create a small group to begin to practice such belonging?

CRAFTING OUR STORIES: MEANING IN MOTION

Stephen Simmons & Bonnie Bates, Authors
Joanne P. Marchetto, Editor

"I think, when you're writing a book, or writing a film, or just living your life, what makes something interesting to other people—what makes a good story—also makes your life into a good story."

—*Caroline**

Of eyes that vainly crave the light, of the objects mean, of the struggle ever renew'd,

Of the poor results of all, of the plodding and sordid crowds I see around me,

Of the empty and useless years of the rest, with the rest me intertwined,

The question, O me! So sad, recurring—What good amid these, O me, O life?

Answer.

That you are here—that life exists and identity,

That the powerful play goes on, and you may contribute a verse.

—Walt Whitman, quoted (in part) by *Arianna**

"I learn by going where I have to go."

—Theodore Roethke

STEVE'S STORY

When I used to go to concerts, including rock concerts, they were pretty orderly (even if they didn't always seem so at the time). You knew exactly where you were supposed to sit or stand, when you were supposed to clap and/or sing along, and who the performers were. It was a performance, and you were the audience. And then, a few years ago, I went to a Dave Matthews Band concert with my younger son. The glow sticks and beach balls showed up, the audience began to sing along with all the songs, people were physically picked up and passed around, and what was happening onstage became just one part of something bigger. This wasn't simply a performance; it was an event. The line between being part of an appreciative audience and being part of the creative flow of the moment had largely vanished. For me, this heralded a trend that has only increased over time—especially with the proliferation of online platforms for artists, musicians, and writers. Everyone is now a content creator, and the lines between author/composer, performance/piece, and audience have become irretrievably blurred. Even God is no longer *the* Creator, and the work is never finished, nor is it necessarily a coherent whole. Mash-up and sampling, cut and paste, are the order of the day. By the same token, there is no such thing as "*the* Creation," since creation is an activity, not a thing. Meaning is belonging and journeying is the goal.

A. Growing Up with Harry and Hermione

Our team wanted to learn about the ways our conversation partners' values shaped their outlooks on the world. To get at this, we asked them, "**Tell me about your favorite story, novel, video game, film, or song.**" While we didn't want to presume that everyone had a religious background, we understood that people everywhere use stories to share and communicate values, traditions, and experiences. With this in mind, we wanted to offer an open question that would help us learn about the stories our conversation partners valued and the ways these stories impacted their experiences. In their answers, many went beyond specific cultural "products" to talk more generally about artists, genres, and group experiences in which they had participated.

It came as no surprise that our respondents' favorites spanned a wide variety of media and niche markets (which is to say that many of their choices were relatively obscure, having a small but dedicated following). The stories with the most mentions included J.K. Rowling's *Harry Potter* series and J.R.R. Tolkien's *Lord of the Rings*. Otherwise, people largely followed the dictum "my playlist, *c'est moi*," with their aesthetic preferences being unique to their own personalities. It was clear from respondents' comments that the forms of culture in which they immersed themselves had strongly shaped and reflected their attitudes toward both the world and their own identities. Their stories were interwoven with significant events in their lives—marriage, having children, divorce, and, for some people, physical or psychological trauma. For example, a number noted that they had basically grown up in parallel with the characters in *Harry Potter*.

As we have seen in their answers to other questions, our conversation partners' preferences tended to favor experience, relationships, personal agency, and engagement over abstract or symbolic meaning. There was little expressed need to make the story, game, or song fit into a "bigger picture" or meta narrative. The story was not about anything except itself, and one had to make choices, often with enormous consequences, based on nothing but one's own gut sense of right and wrong. We saw many variations on the theme *Life just happens, with all its ups and downs, and the point is to live it as fully as one can*. As *Georgia** said about the game *Mass Effect*:

At the very end of this three-game saga, there's this huge choice to be made that just defines everything that's happened through the entire series. It's a very moralistic dilemma because there's really no good option. You're kind of choosing what *you* think would be the best for the entire universe. So I would say that [the game developers] really get me and because of the choice you can play it multiple times and get different outcomes, so...

There may be a transcendent theme in their responses, but it does not have a religious dimension. In the stories they shared, there is no such thing as a divine intervention, or something or someone invading the action in the story from the outside. It is the frame itself that is endlessly susceptible to change. If anything, the transcendent takes the form of technology in computer games and science fiction, and magic in fantasy. People also mentioned "escape" from the world with no particular destination in mind. *Samuel** described transcendence in this way:

> When I was growing up, I grew up in an abusive family situation, so I've always gravitated to anything that was as far away from reality, and I still do. Anything that I watch or read or play, the less it has to do with the real world, the better. I lived through Harry Potter's escape and experienced his situation vicariously.

Whether embraced or resisted, temporality and contingency are the order of the day. *Bethany** said, "Anything can happen at any point in your life and you want to be able to own it and continue on with it, no matter what, so..." Or, as *Sophia** put it, "That's how life works, it's always going back and forth, there's no permanent feeling, no feeling is final, it's just a fine line. So, yeah." People also spoke of how this view of life enabled them to enjoy and feel a sense of wonder toward the little things and moments that make up our days. *Jacob** mentioned *The Little Prince* and mused about "not being able to admire the beauty in things and observing how people can ponder and focus on having power and losing the smaller things in life because of being focused on that."

B. Flexible Belonging

Our conversation partners placed high importance on the value of belonging, but on what might be called flexible belonging: participating in something as long as it suits your needs. You can be intensely involved, and you can also walk away from it. In flexible belonging, you are not striving for perfect attendance; you don't want to be tied down. What often gave them some sense of grounding and comfort was their relationships with family or a small group of friends—again, as in *Harry Potter* and *The Lord of the Rings*. As *Aliyah** put it, "My favorite story, I would say, is *our* love story." Participating in sports teams (either as a player or fan) and, in a somewhat different sense, being one of the participants in a play or concert, provided a similar sense of connection and belonging, even if only a transient one. Still, as powerful as the momentary sense of connection with others at an event may have been, there often remained a tension between belonging and the sense of being a separate and autonomous self. Our respondents want to belong to a community without being absorbed or incorporated into it. Sociologist Zygmunt Bauman has drawn a useful distinction between communities that are momentary and aesthetic, and those that are sustained and ethical, in nature. He writes:

> As long as it stays alive (that is, as long as it is being experienced), aesthetic community is shot through with

a paradox: Since it would betray or refute the freedom of its members were it to claim non-negotiable credentials, it has to keep its entrances and exits wide open. But were it to advertise the resulting lack of binding power, it would fail to perform the reassuring role which for the faithful was their prime motive in joining it.[1]

For a number of respondents, participation in a musical group or theatrical troupe provided a means of being connected to others in an emotionally satisfying, flexible, and creative way:

> What always stuck with me about music is that when you perform and when you sing in general, it's like opening up this part of yourself [she moves her hand away from her heart], so this is the part that people don't see, and the only way to express it or to share it with them is to share it through some sort of medium like singing or music.
>
> —*Petra**

> It's scripted, but you can still just interact with each other, no matter what's going on. It changes.
> —*Mia** (speaking of performing in *Godspell*)

This sense of connected independence was epitomized by Delilah* who said of the film Love, Actually:

> I just like hearing the different circumstances and how everybody develops in those stories and how so many different stories can be occurring so close together at the same time.

C. The Spider-Man Conundrum

i. Trying to Live a Responsibly Normal (but Heroic) Life in the Multiverse

Poor Peter Parker. On one level, he just wants to be a regular guy, but fate, and his father's pioneering (or misguided?) lab experiments, keep pushing him to save the world as cosmic threats keep coming out of left field. What, for him, qualifies as a "normal" life? And who is *he* in the midst of it all? One reason that many of our respondents resonated with the Marvel Comics Universe was their strongly expressed desire, like Peter's, both to experience this beautiful but threatened world and to improve it, to leave a legacy of which they could be proud. Many spoke of wanting to work for social justice, especially for the inclusion and acceptance of oppressed and marginalized people, although there were few suggestions of concrete strategies for accomplishing this.

Our conversation partners often referenced favorites in which the main character was an outlier in one way or another, as they had felt themselves to be, and in which diversity was depicted as a positive and even necessary factor in meeting whatever challenge presented itself. As one put it, speaking of the Marvel Cinematic Universe:

> So yeah, all these people being brought together with different strengths, different weaknesses, different philosophies of life, but working together to save the world for all, I think is pretty awesome.
>
> —*Ethan**

Some of our respondents self-identified as privileged. While they had received certain advantages by reason of education, race, and class, they saw themselves as working in solidarity with others to make a path through an unpredictable and often threatening world:

> The singer is telling us—or whoever is listening—like, come on, you can get up, you can move on, we all need saving, we all have hard times, and it's dark and scary but you have to make it through.
> —*Chloe** (speaking of Jon McLaughlin's song "We All Need Saving")

Again, as noted earlier, the emphasis here is on the value of living in the present moment, whatever may lie in the past or arrive in the future. While there may be some nostalgia for happy endings, there is little anticipation of one at the end of the story. The story may not even have an ending at all, other than doing a kind of fade-out.

While there may be some nostalgia for happy endings, there is little anticipation of one at the end of the story. The story may not even have an ending at all other than doing a kind of fade-out.

Many of the songs referred to by our conversation partners mentioned the themes of living from moment to moment and coping with whatever comes. If there is a "quest," it is for the quest itself, and the companions one meets along the way are what matter. There is no need for a goal or an objective. *Genesis**, referring to the game *Mass Effect*, said,

> You just keep going through it, and no matter how you play the game, the end result is that the command ship and the universe explodes. No matter what you do, the

same thing happens. All that you are determining is what color the explosion is.

ii. Identity, Values, and Nostalgia

As might be expected, some of our conversation partners expressed a sense of anxiety and weariness at constantly having to reinvent themselves in a culture where everything seems to be changing. There are few or no agreed-upon rules or fixed points of reference, and "end of the world" scenarios abound. A number of respondents cited films like *It's a Wonderful Life*, *The Sound of Music*, and *The Wizard of Oz* as providing a nostalgic link to the past. Several of our conversation partners expressed a longing for a more settled time in which identity and values were simply "given" and community was not something to be achieved but inherited.

Interestingly, nostalgia plays a significant role among both faith communities and nones and dones, similarly encouraging feeling and a sense of connectedness without demanding a particular response or commitment. In *Atlas of the Heart*, Brené Brown discusses how we have understood nostalgia:

> Nostalgia was considered a medical disease and a psychiatric disorder until the early nineteenth century. Today, researchers describe nostalgia as a frequent, primarily positive, context-specific bittersweet emotion that combines elements of happiness and sadness with a sense of yearning and loss. The researchers also tell us that feeling nostalgic involves putting ourselves at the center of a story in which we're reminiscing about people we are close to or about important events in our lives. Interestingly, nostalgia is more likely to be triggered by negative moods, like loneliness, and by our struggles to find meaning in our current lives.[2]

There is a longing, explicit or implicit, for "the good old days" (in Peter Parker's case, think of his beloved Aunt May), when things were supposedly simpler and more coherent than they are perceived to be now. In our conversations, we often heard that millennials and Gen Z are tired of struggling with vocation, family relationships, anxiety about the future, and so on. There is a tension between an insistence on self-determination and a desire to find a place to "be." While our conversation partners didn't want to be constrained or held captive by the past, they did yearn for a solid place to stand as they charted their own way. As *Fiona** put it:

While our conversation partners didn't want to be constrained or held captive by the past, they did yearn for a solid place to stand as they charted their own way.

> So for me, you know, it's light lead the way, trust your moral instincts, do what makes you feel good, do what brings the light outside you to share it with people.

iii. The Big Story?

Perhaps the question for all of us is *Where is the light to be found?* For Christian types, it's best to tread softly here. It is quite tempting at this point to say something like, "In Jesus Christ, the light of the world." And that is precisely the kind of thing we tried to avoid in our conversations. While our partners knew that we all are members of faith communities, we tried to be scrupulous about not bringing the Christian story, or any "big story" as a kind of punchline or clincher, into the discussion. We came with the understanding that for this group there *is* no big story, except perhaps in the "intratextual" way that shows up in the Marvel comics and films, the *Harry Potter* series, or *The Lord of the Rings*. While an earlier generation had endless discussions over whether the protagonist in *Cool Hand Luke* or *One Flew Over the Cuckoo's Nest* was in any sense a Christ figure, this kind of thing was completely lacking in our conversations. There was no felt need to connect with religious symbolism or look through or behind anything to find a deeper meaning. If *The Lord of the Rings* is about the Christian story in any sense, it is an oblique one that echoes the themes of many other mythologies and sagas—something that our conversation partners found very congenial. As *Madison** put it, commenting on Neil Gaiman's *American Gods*:

> He does a lot with classic literature and mythology and pulls a lot of different genres in, and really tells classic stories in a new way. He likes to play with different pantheons and gods, and things like that... and what happens when the gods are forgotten and what happens when gods are no longer worshipped and what if these gods are like actual deities that exist and how does our relationship to them affect their existence, and—I don't know. Those are the kinds of things I like to think about and, I just... well, I like to think about them, so... And it's fiction, so it's just... yeah.

Zoey* has the following to say about the book *If Women Rose Rooted: A Journey to Authenticity and Belonging* by Sharon Blackie:

> It's about place and belonging and all those things that I'd been reaching for for so long and going down rabbit-holes to find. She tells these really cool mythical stories, based in Celtic mythology, but then she zooms back out to her narrative, her story, and also other women's stories about

finding their place and their belonging and it's not one answer, one direct path, but many paths.

In this connection, it is worth noting that both *Lord of the Rings* and *Harry Potter* were written by authors who were quite clear about their Christian commitment, but neither work wears its Christianity on its sleeve in the way that, for instance, *The Lion, the Witch, and the Wardrobe* does. J.R.R. Tolkien and C.S. Lewis, who were close friends, argued vigorously over the role, if any, of allegory in literature.[3]

D. Forming Our Stories

In comparing the reflections of our conversation partners with our own, and broadly speaking, the "church's," stories without simply conflating them, we find a helpful framework in religion scholar James F. Hopewell's book, *Congregation: Stories and Structure*. Adapting Northrop Frye's theory of literary types, Hopewell sought to describe the worldviews of congregations—the ways in which they constitute and orient themselves as communities of faith in terms of the "big story" of the Bible, and other stories as well, as we will discuss in a moment.

As is often noted, faith communities are "story-formed," and we believe that it is at the intersection of stories that the richest conversations may be generated. It is telling that *community* came up as a consistent theme in our discussions. Community is a value that our respondents both highly prized and found strangely elusive. Hopewell's ideas may help us to focus more clearly on points of

> **Faith communities are "story-formed," and we believe that it is at the intersection of stories that the richest conversations may be generated.**

congruence and divergence in the kinds of community represented by the church and those that are described, explicitly or implicitly, by our conversation partners. According to Hopewell, narratives can be grouped (if loosely) into four main types: the gnostic, the charismatic, the canonic, and the empiric. We might identify more with these corresponding classifications of the comic, the romantic, the tragic, and the ironic, respectively.

- **Comic (Gnostic)**—Everything will have a happy ending, with crisis moving to harmony, problem to solution.

- **Romantic (Charismatic)**—The emphasis here is on transcendence, and on a willingness to enter into a spiritual adventure with the understanding that the main character may discover powers, both internal and external, that don't "fit" the natural world.

- **Tragic (Canonic)**—Everything is in the hands of fate, God's will as expressed in scripture, or some other inescapable force. The script is written in advance, and all one can do is submit to it.

- **Ironic (Empiric)**—There is no preordained or inherent pattern to things; they just *are*, and the best one can do is to take them as they come and cope as one can. One's only consolation is to be found in the companionship one shares with others along the way.

Hopewell points out that many stories are actually hybrids—comic ironies, tragic romances, or romantic tragedies. In fact, we might note that few works of either classic literature or contemporary media are pure examples of any one type. In *Macbeth*, Shakespeare injects the comedic drunken porter scene to lighten the mood and, in a way, to make the horror all the more horrific. The *Indiana Jones* movies, which are essentially romantic (what could be more so than a new search for the Ark of the Covenant or the Holy Grail?), inject touches like Jones's comic fear of snakes or his ironic relationship with Short Round to let us know that the action is not entirely serious.

Only the combinations of polar opposites—comedy and tragedy, and romance and irony—are structurally impossible. For instance, "Gnostic and charismatic (comedic and romantic) approaches assume the spontaneous inner energy of the known world, whether in the cosmos itself (the gnostic view) or by active spirit, as the charismatic view has it."[4] It is also important to note that, for Hopewell, none of the categories is more inherently "Christian" than the others. Congregations, and people within congregations, may exhibit characteristics of all four. This may help to account for latent and overt conflict within and between churches; there are clashes, not only between personalities, but also between worldviews—the way we understand how the world works, and how we tell stories to explain what we know to be true.

The two categories that would seem to typify many of our responses are the ironic and, to a lesser extent, the comic. In some cases, as in the Marvel movies, there is an interesting tension between romantic and ironic elements where the drama is played out in grand scale, but the interaction among the characters involves a lot of bickering, ribbing, and earthy humor by way of keeping it real. As previously noted, when the comic predominates, problems tend to be resolved in the end, even if there's little evidence except what is known after the fact. Our conversation partners often expressed an intuition that "somehow

For the most part, what predominated was an ironic sense that "whatever happens, we're in this together."

things will work out." Their stories were not romantic in the sense of seeking transcendent meaning beyond the present situation, nor were they tragic, looking ahead with the expectation of some kind of eschatological fulfillment for justification or validation. For the most part, what predominated was an ironic sense that "whatever happens, we're in this together."

E. The Power of Responsible Storytelling

If it seems strange to use this framework to discuss biblical narratives, it is worth noting that, as religion scholar Richard Swanson puts it, before Bible stories were Bible stories, they were *stories*—and, as he says, public stories. "These old stories come out of painful and complicated worlds and represent valiant attempts to engage that pain and complication, to wrestle with it rather than to retreat from it."[5]

At times, the church has taught that there is one singular meaning or interpretation of biblical stories, which only needs to be "decoded." This singular interpretation is known in advance, and this method precludes asking uncomfortable questions. In this way, while the intent is to honor biblical narratives, the actual effect is to enclose them in a kind of protective bubble or Teflon coating that keeps them from living and breathing in the present moment. Stories from the broader culture, in contrast, have no such immunization, and so may be considered fair game. Ironically, the Bible may recover its function as a proclamation and critique (often enough of the church itself) when biblical stories are treated as partners in an ongoing conversation. In this way, we can learn from all our conversation partners and become cocreators in interpretation and discovery. We can be more nuanced in storytelling with new interpretation, values, and meaning. Indeed, when we learn to tell our own stories via other cultural products in such a no-holds-barred way, we may rediscover the power of biblical narrative itself.[6]

Providing a setting in which persons both inside and outside the church can discuss a variety of stories on such a level playing field could be a powerful way of vivifying biblical narratives for both groups, including those for whom they have become old hat and those for whom they are completely new. In addition, the formation of an open storytelling group could create a powerful platform for "creatives" to exercise their gifts as an expression of their discipleship. Jim and Janet Stahl have worked with small storytelling groups around the globe. Their experiences highlight the value of oral, communal storytelling:

> While living on Epi Island, Vanuatu, my wife and I started collecting what are known as *custom* stories from adults in the Lamen language group. Custom stories are traditional stories that have been passed on from generation to generation. The Lamen language community is mostly an oral community and although a multilingual community they use their own language, Lamen, when telling stories to each other. Most of the stories we collected had to do with the origins of Epi and Lamen Islands. Much to our surprise, none of the stories were the same. Our assumption was that if not the same, they would be very close to being so. We assumed oral memory would equate to a verbatim retelling. In reading *Orality and Literacy* by Walter J. Ong, I came to a section that made me reflect back on our experience on Epi Island learning the Lamen language and culture: "In all cases, verbatim or not, oral memorization is subject to variation from direct social pressures. Narrators narrate what audiences call for or will tolerate."[7]

Biblical stories were originally transmitted orally and were shaped in the light of the way ordinary people told and heard them. Why should we do any less?

F. Summary

For our respondents, no stories are canonical, and none has privileged status. Respect and attention must be earned. Biblical stories compete in the same arena as other cultural products and are evaluated by the same criteria; most of all, they need to be congruent with one's own sense of self. People in the church need not only to "know" the biblical stories, but also to absorb, digest, and practice them.

By the same token, nones and dones do not recognize a distinction between sacred art and secular art. The same subject matter can be serious, profane, the object of parody, etc., depending on the use the artist makes of it. What matters is what the work evokes in the audience.

For a faith community, believers embody and enact values that ultimately come from a transcendent source such as God, one's own Buddha nature, etc. For our conversation partners, values are understood to come from the self, family, and friends. There is very little reliance on society or large institutions for the impartation and perpetuation of values. If anything, these entities are to be regarded with a critical eye, if not with outright skepticism. In everyday life, our conversation partners determined that institutions can be largely irrelevant.

While faith communities are "story-formed," the stories remain constant. They can have multiple interpretations and meanings, but there is a core tradition that can be adapted and interpreted within limits. This tradition remains the center around which belief and practice gravitate. For our respondents, the formation of community by stories is a matter of momentary affinity, with the understanding that such communities are transitory, with appeals to authority or group loyalty judged to be manipulative or, at best, irrelevant.

Religious communities tend to be text-based. It is worth noting that the proliferation of Bible translations and Bible-based materials in multimedia formats in recent decades has left the text itself under negotiation in a way that wasn't the case when the King James Version was the Bible for English-speaking Christians. Nones and dones appreciate many different forms of story and drink equally from various media wells. The experience is the value, whether it occurs in the "real world," online, or through other media.

With these observations in mind, we suggest some strategies for promoting generative conversations between faith communities and people (including those within our congregations) who find "God talk" increasingly boring, constricting, or simply meaningless:

- Return to telling and performing the story rather than reading the text; give people the chance to act out the story, and to go "off script" in creative ways.

- Adopt an improvisational, open-ended approach to scriptural passages that lets them speak for themselves rather than looking for a predictable "punchline" or outcome.

- Show an openness to a diversity of artistic expressions, including both works with explicitly religious themes and works that are more secular in nature.

- Be willing to explore and discuss works of art, film, novels, video games, or music that are deliberately "transgressive" and that push the envelope of religious concepts. People are engaging them!

- Encourage people to create their own artistic expressions; cultivate the art of the amateur.

- Be willing to leave things "granular" or episodic, rather than having an overarching theme or leading to a foregone conclusion. The basic approach is exploratory rather than explanatory. Parables, Hasidic and Sufi stories, Zen koans and tales, and the like are useful here.

G. For Further Group Discussion

1. Share your favorite piece of media (book, film, TV show, song, video game, etc.) and how it has shaped who you are today.

2. How do the stories from your favorite piece of media inform or connect with your personal story?

3. What pieces of media bring you comfort, and why?

4. Throughout our preparation of this book, we were immersed in numerous different media that shared stories that stretched, discomforted, and challenged us to grow. What stories offend you or make you uncomfortable? How can those stories lead you to deeper growth?

5. In this chapter, we have drawn a distinction between "flexible belonging" and making a firm and lasting commitment to another person or group. What examples of these kinds of affiliation can you think of in your own life? Have some of them changed from one to the other over time?

6. In line with the Peter Parker/Spider-Man conundrum, how does one live a responsible life in an increasingly abnormal world? To whom do you hold yourself accountable? As in the musical *Hamilton*, who tells your story? Who writes the ending?

BRAVING THE STORMS

James Stahl & Joanne P. Marchetto, Authors
Janet Stahl, Editor

"So it [my adversity] allowed me to kind of slow down and just like take a breath and figure it out."

*—Jessica**

"You should never view your challenges as a disadvantage. Instead, it's important for you to understand that your experience facing and overcoming adversity is actually one of your biggest advantages."

—Michelle Obama, 2016 City College of New York
commencement speech

"My brothers and sisters, whenever you face trials of any kind, consider it nothing but joy, because you know that the testing of your faith produces endurance; and let endurance have its full effect, so that you may be mature and complete, lacking in nothing. If any of you is lacking in wisdom, ask God, who gives to all generously and ungrudgingly, and it will be given you."

—James 1:2–5 (NRSV)

JIM'S STORY

I lived in Vanuatu for 15 years researching Vanuatu languages and helping with literacy and translation efforts. Vanuatu is a small island country between Fiji and Australia. While there, I contracted dengue fever. Dengue is a mosquito-borne disease that occurs in periodic outbreaks, and usually in cities. There are no vaccines or prophylaxis to take for dengue. The fever is known as the "bone-crusher," as one feels like one's bones are going to break. It often comes with a rash and serious eye pain. The fever intensifies and gradually recedes over the course of two weeks. It also leads to temporary depression and irritability. My doctor in Vanuatu told me to get lots of rest, drink lots of water, and take copious amounts of Tylenol.

So, there are four strains of dengue, and if you get one, you become immune to it. However, if you get a certain combination of strains, you run the risk of what is known as dengue-hemorrhagic fever, or DHF. Not good. People can dehydrate and die from this. I had dengue twice, and I now run the risk of getting the dreaded third combination that can lead to DHF, because my job takes me to places where dengue is endemic. I can resort to worrying about the possibility of getting dengue again but choose to continue traveling and do what I can to prevent it. If I get dengue again, hopefully I can stay hydrated and get the help and rest I need. I have carried on working in tropical parts of the world where mosquito-borne diseases are prevalent and have learned to manage the risk and continue to do what I love. I've learned that life doesn't promise to be disease-free despite our best efforts and retreating is not my choice.

JOANNE'S STORY

I grew up in a very ordinary, average, middle-class home. My parents were the children of immigrants, and they were realizing the "American dream." My mother was the first person to graduate from high school. My father joined the navy during the Vietnam War. My grandfather purchased our first family home with the aid of the GI Bill. They were hard workers who also had to face hardships. My grandmother lived with schizophrenia her entire life, and we lived with my grandparents. My parents struggled to pay the bills, but somehow we managed to "make it" each month.

When I was a senior in high school, I was on track to graduate at the top of my class, receiving a handful of scholarships, and admission to my number one university. Within months, my life completely changed. Our country went into recession. It was after school one afternoon when my parents sat us down in the living room and explained that we were going to lose our home. We weren't sure how long we had; we didn't know when we would have to leave. The house, my father's business, and all the money he worked so hard to build—gone.

I was 17 years old and scrappy, and I believed education and hard work would be enough. I did all the "right" things: I got my driver's license, a job, and an application to community college. I could not afford the university education price tag. My mother moved without my father; the two of them separated shortly after the news. My mother blamed my father for what happened. My grandfather was diagnosed with terminal cancer and died within months. I needed to find a place to live and a roommate. I soon learned that not everyone is born with the same opportunities and that race, class, and immigration status all play a role in your ability to be approved for food stamps. I saw the holes in the American dream. I had to shut down my emotions or I would not have survived this period of my life. I went into survival mode. I looked for escape. I longed for a community of people that I could go to for support or advice. This is the same time I felt rejected by the church of my childhood. As my family fell apart, we no longer had a place where we belonged. I had to figure out how I would face the biggest challenge of my life.

A. Facing Adversity

We all face adversity in our lives; these challenges shape our identity, relationships, and choices. We asked our conversation partners: "Tell us about a challenge or a missed opportunity that has shaped who you are today." Our team wanted to learn how they faced struggles, worked through conflict, or lived with their regrets. We wondered: *Did they make meaning out of the difficulties they faced?* Many of the conversation partners responded by telling us their experiences or stories.

Storytelling is a fascinating part of our existence and being, and it permeates every part of our lives and society. We all have individual and collective stories to tell. Our stories, especially our stories of deep emotional pain, struggle, and experience of adversity, make us human. Sharing our stories of adversity builds empathy and connection.

Frequently, the conversation partners articulated their stories of challenging experiences with a moral, or a lesson learned. Several people said something like, "I believe that everything happens for a reason," or stated that they felt that—despite the adversity they had faced—they are where they're supposed to be. What we didn't hear were any stories of deep-seated anger, desire for revenge, or withdrawal from the world. This group learned not only how to cope but also gained wisdom. We learned that they moved through these experiences and developed resiliency. They shared stories of resources, relationships, and values that empowered them through these times of conflict and change. They shared wisdom for moving through difficult times.

i. University or Job Choice Challenge

Our conversation partners shared stories of challenges in their careers, personal lives, and relationships. Many people were challenged by a change in career paths; what they intended to do was not what they ended up doing. *Leeanne** struggled with the "toxic" environment of her job, but it led her on a different path. Many people seemed fine in hindsight with changes to the plan for their lives. This was reflected in the comment by *Aiden** that "it was a good experience, even though it sucked." *Lucy** received a scholarship to a college that was far away, and she was looking forward to new experiences when her parents put a down payment on tuition at a school close to home. While disappointed at first, she was thankful to attend the local school; she even hated to admit that her mom was right. Many people described challenges that revolved around the transitions in life from high school to college or workforce, or job-to-job transitions.

ii. Sports Dreams

Some respondents were athletes who sustained injuries; others wished they had been more involved in sports in school, and still others were less involved in sports and more involved in studies. A significant portion wished they had worked or studied more diligently in school. Athletics gave a sense of belonging in community, while they also presented a set of challenges: *José** expressed a sense of feeling alive while playing sports and wished he had challenged himself to work harder. *Frank** shared a sense of joy in basketball and regrets that he had given it up. *Rachel** told about a softball injury that changed the entire course she had planned for her life. For them, sports created a sense of belonging, but also left them wondering what *could have been* if things had been different.

iii. Family Conflict

Divorce and family relationships were discussed by almost one-third of our conversation partners (31 percent). Many people discussed the impact of their parents' separation and divorce on their lives. Others shared their own experience of going through a divorce. *Lily** shared her personal divorce story, and she beautifully described the tribe of friends that surrounded her during this challenging time. Reflecting on this story, she was "glad to have gone through this difficult experience" because she discovered she was able to "rise to the challenge." *Theresa** shared her story of living through a "very ugly" custody battle and how her experience broke down the myth of the importance of "staying together." *Christine** was grateful to get to know her parents as individuals after they had divorced.

Given that our conversation partners' ages fell between 18 and 39 years old, some of the situations they described seemed to be those that many people experience during those years of life: choosing educational and vocational pathways, finding a partner, and raising a family. Unlike earlier generations, our conversation partners did not express a description of financial windfalls, moving into an upscale community, or living a posh lifestyle as part of their "better" path or life. This generation is less wealthy than their parents. Some continue to live with the huge economic burdens of school loans, working multiple jobs to meet expenses. In answering this question, our conversation partners did not talk about money; they did not discuss finances as a challenge and/or missed opportunity. Perhaps if we had asked about finances we would have heard more about this topic.

iv. Mental Health

Our conversation partners were open and honest in sharing personal stories of their mental health. *Tim** shared a story of the process of learning to accept himself as he addressed his mental health, addictive tendencies, and coming out. *Heidi** was open about living with ADHD, and *Kayla** shared a story of living with anxiety and depression. Others shared about the importance of relationships, community, and recovery groups as a place of belonging and growth. A key learning from our conversation partners was that poor mental health is a part of life to be accepted in ourselves and others, and it is not a challenge to be overcome. *Taylor** shared his grieving the death of someone close to him and that he noticed behavior changes in other family members because of the loss. Addressing his grief and being honest about his friend's depression helped him be "empathetic about others' trauma." It is true, as Michelle Obama said, that "Grief and resilience live together."[1] Several people noted how they were moving forward after facing adversity or a missed opportunity.

A key learning from our conversation partners was that poor mental health is a part of life to be accepted in ourselves and others, and it is not a challenge to be overcome.

For many, adverse situations helped them develop confidence and resilience, as well as the ability to empathize with others and their trauma.

B. Developing Resiliency

The overarching theme our conversation partners shared was that they learned resilience by going through challenges in life. While facing adversity was deeply painful, and many described distressing struggles, they faced these trials. They shared their learning and personal growth as well as the resources that had helped them through such difficult times. As *Tammy** narrated her story of leaving a problematic relationship, she explained that her mother was a resource she could lean on and a source of advice. Family "helped along the way" as *Tim** worked through his mental health and accepted his sexuality. Family and friends were the "comfort zone" for *Brian** and he challenged himself to break out and start a new life. Family, counselors, and clergy offered him "support" as he moved through the process of divorce. However, there were conversation partners who did not have family relationships or support, or whose primary struggle was with their family. After one of our conversation partners, *Lauren**, was in an accident, she had no family resources to rely on, and she struggled to have any kind of family relationships.

Networks and small groups of close friends were a resource for many of our conversation partners. Childhood friends and trusted work colleagues became like family. Several mentioned the resources and support of recovery groups and 12-step programs. These resources empowered people to navigate adversity while holding on to their values. Our conversation partners demonstrated a willingness to learn from their mistakes and grow through adversity.

Facing fear was a factor in many stories. As *Octavia** shared her story, she said, "If your dreams don't scare you, then they're not big enough. And I'm like, well, I know my dreams are real big because I'm terrified." For *Sophia**, fear held her back in choosing a school to attend. In finding a job, *Grace** worked through the fear and anxiety of the unknown. Others, like *Emery**, stated that it's good to get out of one's comfort zone. However, some of the conversation partners chose options that seemed safer than others. *Phoebe** described herself as risk averse and wondered what might have happened had she chosen the riskier alternative. *Brian**, who broke out of his comfort zone, related that he still lives with fears.

C. Empowering Resources

According to the American Psychological Association, resilience is the ability to bounce back and grow personally after a major life event, conflict, trauma, or serious health problem.[2] Many conversation partners mentioned the phrase "moving forward" and expressed that they had found contentment and fulfillment in their new situations. They showed resilience and growth from their challenges and difficulties.

While one of our conversation partners mentioned the "trendiness" of trauma, most did not share this response. Many people describe unsettling or upsetting events as "traumatic," even though they may not be defined as trauma-inducing experiences. The official definition of trauma, according to the American Psychological Association, "is an emotional response to a terrible event such as an accident, rape, or natural disaster."[3] People react differently to a traumatic event, with responses that include denial, shock, anger, sadness, and/or withdrawal. The majority of our conversation partners were resilient and able to grow through their challenges, which were, by and large, not traumatic events. By staying connected to family and friends, these relationships and resources helped them manage difficult situations more effectively.

Many of our conversation partners described their challenges as experiences where they were able to find their own voice, get over their shyness, or confront a difficult situation. They discovered their own capacity to build resilience. Many, including *Mia**, *Camilla**, *Ella**, *Mila**, *Kinsley**, and *Hadley**, ended their story with the phrase *I am where I am supposed to be*. Some, including *Julian** and *Heather**, shared a sense of discovery or gratitude for the learning and growth that resulted from their adversarial experience. Many conversation partners described the lessons they learned, like becoming more self-aware, empathetic, or humble. *John**, *Willow**, *Arianna**, *Daniella**, and *Nova** all discussed having more confidence in themselves to handle unexpected future challenges.

A fair number of people talked about using therapy and appreciating counselors who helped them through the challenge. It appears that this generation has more social freedom to express failure or weakness and to seek professional counseling than previous generations did. The American Psychiatric Association reported in 2019 that Gen Zers were more likely to have received treatment or gone to therapy (37 percent) than millennials (35 percent), Gen Xers (26 percent), baby boomers (22 percent), and the silent generation (15 percent)."[4] Gen Zers are more open to seeking help and discussing mental health issues and less concerned about it as a stigma than previous generations.[5] Conversation partners noted that having support groups, family, and friends helped them face adverse situations. *Willow** stated, "If you have one person who believes in you, it's amazing the next steps you can take as a human being." Overall, our conversation partners were open about their challenges and missed opportunities, as noted in other research, especially with Gen Z.

Gen Z is coming of age in a post-9/11 world threatened by polarization, violence, pandemics, and war. Our conversation partners practiced active-shooter drills in school and have reached voting age in the era of the Tea Party, Donald Trump, and the Capitol insurrection. This is the context in which we conducted our interviews. Wars in Iraq, Afghanistan, Syria, and now Ukraine have been part of their lives, as have civil wars, climate change, and refugee crises.

Even though we experience a chaotic world, we can still hope for peace. It is encouraging to us that we see signs that many of the young adults we interviewed have developed resiliency. While we might have different frameworks for facing adversity, resiliency offers hope. For example, as we (Jim and Joanne) address adversity, we often lean on prayer and our faith communities to support us. This reminds us to thank God for being alive and well. Seeing the sun come up means another day to live.

As Amanda Gorman recited at the end of her presidential inauguration poem, *The Hill We Climb*, each day brings hope:

> When day comes we step out of the shade,
> aflame and unafraid

The new dawn blooms as we free it
For there is always light,
if only we're brave enough to see it
If only we're brave enough to be it.[6]

D. The Healing Power of Stories

Richard Mollica, a Harvard Medical School professor of psychiatry, writes in his book *Healing Invisible Wounds*, that:

> Survivors [of trauma] from different parts of the world...
> tell strikingly similar stories of the role played by the
> sun and stars in their survival. Looking up at the heavens they saw something that was eternally unaffected by
> human actions. The stars helped keep them alive while
> they were tortured in reeducation camps or prison cells.
> Every morning the sunrise reminded them that they had
> survived another day.[7]

During the early parts of the Russian invasion of Ukraine, many people prayed that the country would stand to see another day. Ukrainian journalists who stayed in Kyiv would tweet daily about the sun rising there, that Ukraine was still Ukrainian, and that seeing the sun and a new day inspired hope. The heavenly bodies inspire hope. Yet for many there is no hope.

As individuals, at times we feel insignificant; world events tempt us to become numb to the chaos. Yet our stories help us and link us to each other and encourage us to hope. In *The Gates of the Forest*, Elie Wiesel concludes a tragic and miraculous story set during World War II with the line, "God made [people] because [God] loves stories."[8] In another of his books, *Messengers of God*, Wiesel writes of "Job: Our Contemporary" as a character from possibly one of the oldest stories in the Bible, and a legendary figure whose story is relevant to our own current stories.[9] While many religious teachers focus on Job's endurance and reward, Wiesel focuses on Job's struggle with God. "Job personified [humanity's] eternal quest for justice and truth—

> **Our stories help us and link us to each other and encourage us to hope.**

he did not choose resignation. Thus, [Job] did not suffer in vain; thanks to him, we know that it is given to [humanity] to transform divine injustice into human justice and compassion."[10]

Mollica states: "When the traumatized inner self is thrown into chaos by violence, spirituality can prevent a total disintegration of the person."[11] He gives the example of Nelson Mandela, who—when released from 27 years of prison and hard labor—did not seek vengeance on his captors but worked for reconciliation. He and thousands of others "revealed similar extraordinary levels of resiliency as a result of their strong spiritual and political orientation."[12]

E. Developing Resiliency through Storytelling

People find inspiration from others' stories and from sacred stories as well. Janet Stahl led a project for women in one part of South Asia where women faced much adversity and often had few opportunities for education and vocation outside being a housekeeper for their own family. The project connected women from several language groups to tell biblical stories in their languages to foster interest and capacity for translating the Bible into those languages. To connect the stories, both conceptually and linguistically, the women told their own stories that were thematically related to the biblical stories. One story they learned to tell was the book of Ruth, which starts with Naomi and her family becoming refugees in Moab because of a famine in Bethlehem. The South Asian women shared their own famine stories and their heartbreaking situations seeing their children suffer. To prevent secondary trauma from hearing stories of adversity, and to help the women cope with adverse situations, Janet promoted the following five principles gleaned from scholars like Mollica:

1. Listen with compassion.

2. Encourage the expression of emotion.

3. Pray together.

4. Tell an appropriate (Bible) story.

5. Do small acts of kindness for others.[13]

These women, who were initially reticent and shy, became safe havens in their communities, creating opportunities for dialogue across religious lines and offering ways for their neighbors to cope with the challenges they faced. As they shared and listened to one another's stories, the women became catalysts for developing community and spiritual growth.

Janet wrote that the first step for the women was to recognize the behaviors of biblical characters within the stories: "Hannah *cried* frequently and *refused* to eat. Naomi was *angry* or *depressed*, and when the people of Bethlehem came out to greet her, she told them to call her Mara, or *'bitter,'* then she complained to God."[14] The women learned to identify signs of emotional wounds in the biblical characters, and after reflecting on their own experiences, they told stories connected with that pain; it was a point of connection between a personal story and a biblical story. Next, they identified similar behaviors in other people to foster emotional healing. They recognized that the healing process takes time and learned to have compassion toward others wherever they may be in their healing journey. This is an important factor: Healing is a process and a journey. *Aubrey** recounted that she had suffered from PTSD, which caused her to miss out on many opportunities. She is aware of her difficult situation and stated, "I think healing is a process that goes on until you die."

Storytelling and the development of resiliency share several key factors, including being part of a tight-knit community, having a strong faith, and finding meaning in the difficult times of our lives. Mollica writes that telling our stories and listening to others' stories is foundational to developing empathy with others who have experienced trauma. Storytelling helps us connect with people, which helps the one suffering trauma escape their sense of isolation. Storytelling can also be therapeutic to the traumatized person, and enhance their psychological recovery.[15]

The stories we tell each other whether with family, friends, or acquaintances can help us get through difficult times and begin the healing process, encourage patience and empathy, and appreciate others as we in turn listen to their stories. *Kristen** told us how her family supported her and helped her through a very difficult time in her life. She said,

> It took me over a year to actually make the change, and I think it's something that has remained with me for the past couple of years as I've kind of been healing from it. But that was definitely a challenge and I think I definitely leaned on my family in particular and some of my close friends to kind of guide me and help me through that time. My parents and my siblings were very supportive, as were my friends.

Hearing and telling our stories helps us come together and identify who we are—our origins, our values—while at the same time appreciating the stories and values of others, whether we are from South Asia or northeastern Pennsylvania.

F. The Pandemic

The Covid-19 pandemic has been traumatic for some and trying for others.[16] For example, Jim's mother, who is in her 90s, is confined and limited by the constraints of the pandemic and her declining health. She credits her faith for helping her through the trying times. Much of her day is spent reading the Bible and new books, listening to familiar hymns and Gospel music, and reminiscing about family stories, mostly from her childhood, which includes the Great Depression. She likes to tell how her mother was known as someone ready to provide a meal to hungry train travelers who were homeless during that era. She acted generously and in solidarity with others, even though their family was poor themselves. Perhaps those actions shine in her life, and helped her later in life, such as the time she joined with other affected women to bravely walk through a men's club while being harassed in order to get to the polling station to cast their ballots. These are examples of grandparent stories, like those discussed in chapter 1, which help us, as family, to know her character more fully and influence how we handle difficult situations.

The Covid-19 pandemic affected our conversation partners in different ways. *Ariana** found it difficult to balance the demands of having three children at home during the pandemic while she was attending graduate school. *Petra** struggled with anxiety and PTSD due to a car accident and was grateful to be working from home during the pandemic. Because *Georgia** had worked through the anxiety of a conflict with her difficult boss, she appreciated "confronting things about myself... it helped in the last year with the pandemic." *Phoebe** shared reflecting on her fear of having a baby and the grief of a miscarriage: "The pandemic made us rethink things. The challenge of the pandemic and the challenge of the miscarriage did help me learn more about what I do want without letting my fears get in the way."

The majority of those who discussed the pandemic saw it as an opportunity for growth. *Julia** had to scrap everything and change all her plans and goals for her vocation:

> I never would have gotten to do [these things] if it weren't for the pandemic. So even though it did pose a challenge and it did prevent some things from happening, it also opened a new doorway for other opportunities that have made me really happy, and even though I wish I could go back and do those things I missed out on, I'm still happy with where I am right now.

Karen* was "afraid of a lot of things." While she constantly thought about these fears, she said:

> I got scared, although there was no reason. I hadn't lost my job yet... I was fortunate. But I was very scared, and I instantly went back to *Maybe I should just go back home...* Then I thought *Wait a minute. No, I can do this. There's no reason to be scared. Not yet, at least.* I was psyching myself out. I thought back and realized I needed to push myself, just as I thought I should have pushed myself before.

G. Resiliency in Faith Communities: Facing Adversity Together

In the past, churches and faith communities were a resource to help people through difficult times as discussed in chapter 2. I (Joanne) wonder about a shift that appears to be happening in which churches are avoiding challenges. In the churches I have served, in general and across generations, I have heard many people say to me over the past twenty years, "I want to go to church because I want to feel good; I don't want to be challenged." I have often wondered about this. Do people have to hide the adversity they face to not appear "weak" or "less than" others? Are people in church afraid of being judged, or are people using the church as a place of escape?[17] Are faith communities a safe place where I can bring all my struggles in the face of the adversity, so I am able to face a new day? People participate in faith communities for a variety of reasons: comfort, belonging, and escape.

When a faith community experiences adversity, there are different ways people react to the anxiety and stress. Within congregations in conflict, people resort to a series of different emotional patterns when the anxiety is high. These four patterns of emotional reactivity are fight, flight, freeze, or fawn. When the challenges seem insurmountable, some may react with a *fight* response such as bullying, manipulation, name-calling, and acts of violence. People take *flight* by moving church membership or leaving all faith communities. Withholding money and not participating are *freeze* responses. An example of *fawning* is trying to keep people happy or accommodating them when facing adversity.

During the Covid-19 pandemic, congregational anxiety has been high, resulting in added stress and exhaustion for pastors while they are facing many challenges. Pastor Melissa Florer-Bixler identifies many reasons why pastors are resigning from ministry in large numbers: increased hours and anxiety, decreased budgets, political infighting, and a lack of support.[18] These are painful struggles happening in our churches. Florer-Bixler writes:

> It was never our job as pastors to keep the institutional church from dissolving. We are not spiritual entertainers. We didn't take up this work to compete in the market-place of meaning-making. We don't build institutions. The institutional church is an experiment and like all

experiments, it can fail. When it does, we wait in hope to
see what good work God is up to next.[19]

Congregations are facing change and challenges they have
never experienced before. Political scientist and pastor Ryan
P. Burge explores possible causes for the shifting demographics
of church membership and affiliation in *The Nones: Where They
Came From, Who They Are, and Where They Are Going.*[20] He notes
that these challenges are complex, and he identifies factors that
are at play in shifting church affiliation, including secularization,
politics, and the internet.[21] Taking a broader view, he also recognizes that these factors are influenced by the larger, systematic
whole; it is an oversimplification to think we can identify these
problems in order to "fix" the church. We need to look at the
broader world and culture of which the church is a part and discover ways that we can *adapt* to the changes happening in society.
It seems that our society has bought into the idea that the church
is a "crutch" or the "opiate for the masses," whereas a counselor or
12-step group is the place for honest help in coping with life. So...
how can the church develop resiliency in the face of adversity?
How do we develop resources for communities (faith-based and
secular organizations) to support the healing process in working
through challenges and conflict?

Systems theory is a way of thinking through how we manage difficult situations. Pastor and consultant Peter Steinke has
helped church professionals understand the difference between
linear thinking and systems thinking. Linear thinking is cause
and effect: A is the cause, and B is the effect. Systems thinking is
a circular understanding of a problem and potential solutions. A
and B mutually influence each other. For example: My spouse is
angry because I came home late from the office. Linear thinking
says that because of A (coming home late), B results (my spouse
is angry). In a systems view, my spouse and I mutually influence

each other. I am coming home late because I want to avoid an earlier argument we had over the household finances, and my spouse isn't angry only because I came home late. There is residual anger from the earlier argument.

When a problem arises in a congregation, people can be tempted to view the situation with linear thinking. Our brains prefer a simpler solution to the most complex of problems. Cause and effect thinking leads us to believe we can apply quick fixes to resolve the tension and make sense of large challenges and complex problems. The problem is that this often doesn't work because of the multiple factors at work in the emotional system. In congregations facing adversity, emotional relationships are complex and become patterned. The more anxious people become, the more they become divided by conflict and reactive in fight, flight, freeze, or fawn patterns.

A systems view looks to how we mutually influence each other, how the problems and the people are all affected. Conflict mediators, consultants, and coaches can also help in healing and offer support for communities. One possible resource is congregational storytelling, which is an effective way of sharing feelings and experiences so people can connect with one another and build empathy. It is also an effective tool for identifying resources and brainstorming for creative new possibilities for the future.

When working with congregations in conflict, I ask them to tell me their story of who they are and the events that led them to this point of calling in a coach for mediation. While it helps me learn their background, values, and guiding principles, it also reminds them of the shared history, accomplishments, and relationships they have built with one another and their community. Telling their story reminds them of those experiences they were able to work through in the past, and it gives them courage to face their current situation. Their stories remind them of the deep relationships and support they have in one another. Even when they disagree on the problems or the resources needed to solve them, storytelling connects them emotionally, reminds them of their shared values, and guides them through stressful and conflicted times.

Another helpful concept in systems theory is self-differentiation. This is the ability to define oneself, one's core values, mission in life, and principles for decision-making without falling into the reactive patterns of fight, flight, freeze, or fawn. Self-differentiation helps a person develop their self-awareness, stating their own beliefs while not emotionally reacting to another person's thoughts, feelings, or decisions.

Our conversation partners described experiences of managing their own anxiety, and of facing struggles and pain that helped them discover their values and define who they are as individuals (self-differentiation). Some of our conversation partners shared stories in which they struggled to learn new emotional patterns of responding to challenging situations. They shared stories of the resilience, courage, resources, and connections that helped them grow. They were open and honest about mental health, they took risks in finding new careers, they faced challenging health situations and grief. They faced adversity with strength, defining their core values, discovering their identity and capacity for growth. They showed emotional intelligence and awareness that, even through challenge and change, "they were where they were supposed to be." They demonstrated that it is possible to acquire resources and develop new patterns to help us face adversity and develop resilience and strength. Building bridges, engaging in conversations, and sharing stories of adversity across generations can help strengthen relationships, build empathy, and deepen connections.

H. Summary

We saw resiliency in our conversation partners. They were open and honest in sharing their experiences of family, education, challenges in the workplace, and caring for their mental health. They shared their wisdom and learning and showed vulnerability.

Storytelling is healing, connective, and builds resiliency as we face challenges and adversity. Arthur Frank, in his book *The Wounded Storyteller*, offers examples of types of stories that move through the stages of healing. Stories offer role models and alternative choices. They offer an opportunity for people to be in their stories and share their experiences of working through their adversity. For faith communities, the Bible is full of real-life stories of humans struggling, and of God directing them to imagine another way of living. Congregations can create spaces where people can be authentic and honest about their challenges and missed opportunities.

- For the storyteller, the experience can be a catalyst toward healing and self-discovery.

- For the listener, storytelling has the power to build empathy and connection.

There are many resources available for individuals and communities who are working through adversity. Paying attention to the emotional process of congregations is important. These can accompany you on this journey:

- The Lombard Mennonite Peace Center provides tools for congregations to move through conflict. They offer workshops in conflict transformation skills, healthy congregations, and mediation training.[22]

- The development of care teams such as a Stephen Ministry program or a Called to Care team staffed by faith community members can offer support and healing.

- Family and friends are tremendous resources in supporting individuals and congregations through difficult experiences.

- 12-step groups and recovery programs can provide a safe, brave space of mutual support.

- Mental health resources, licensed counselors, spiritual directors, and support groups are good resources to help face adversity.

I. For Further Group Discussion

1. Tell a story of a missed opportunity or challenge that has shaped who you are today.

2. What have you learned from our conversation partners about resiliency? When have you discovered you are resilient?

3. What is your default emotional response to anxiety (fight, flight, freeze, or fawn)? Share an experience in which you reacted in that way (feel free to be playful!). How do you resist this pattern?

4. How has the Covid-19 pandemic shaped the life of your (faith) community? What challenges have you faced?

5. What are your resources (people, communities, emotional supports, grandparent stories) that help you to face adversity? What new resources have you discovered from reading this chapter?

A LEGACY OF GOOD VIBES

Brandon M. Heavner & Janet Stahl, Authors
Joanne P. Marchetto, Editor

"Do you fear death?"

—Davey Jones, *Pirates of the Caribbean: Dead Man's Chest*

"Luke, when gone am I, the last of the Jedi will you be. Luke, the Force runs strong in your family. Pass on what you have learned."

—Yoda, *Star Wars Episode VI: Return of the Jedi*

"The needs of the many outweigh the needs of the few, or the one... I have been, and always shall be, your friend. Live long and prosper."

—Spock, *Star Trek II: The Wrath of Khan*

"The ultimate test of a moral society is the kind of world that it leaves to its children."

—Attributed to Dietrich Bonhoeffer

JANET'S STORY

I have a ceramic bowl on a pedestal in my dining room that was my maternal grandmother's. I am fairly certain it was meant to hold fresh fruit, but I have a potted Christmas cactus in it because my grandmother had a Christmas cactus planted in it in her dining room. I can't say that I think the bowl is particularly beautiful, and I really don't care about its monetary worth, but it evokes memories of delicious Thanksgiving meals with extended family, playing board games with siblings and cousins while my grandmother listened to the radio broadcast of Steelers or Pirates games, and dashing up the alley behind her house to visit her sister, our great aunt, or my paternal grandparents. The bowl is not my grandmother's legacy to me but the symbol that reminds me of the stories of my experiences with my grandmother, and the stories she shared with me of her life experiences. My grandmother's legacies to me are the ties to a family of hard-working, thrifty (but generous), resourceful people who knew the value of singing and laughing together. I hope my legacy is a rich set of stories and memories that remind them they were important to me and inspire them to share love and mercy with others.

AURORA'S* STORY

A couple of years ago I ran into a guy I went to school with, elementary through high school. We were talking and he mentioned a specific memory that he had of me, and I had no recollection of this memory at all. His memory was that he was being transferred to the first- or second-grade class that I happened to be in, but in the middle of the school year. And he said that the first thing that happened when the teacher introduced him to the class was that I spoke up and said, "Hey, why don't you come over and sit with us?" And I kind of became friends with him through that experience. It's funny that he remembered this, and how it really touched him—that it was kind of a big thing for him. And so, I want people to remember me like that. I want to be remembered as the person who will invite you over to my table and take you in.

BRANDON'S STORY

My family has owned and operated a small-grains and beef cattle farm for generations. I spent my youth feeding the beef stock, maintaining fencing, and operating all kinds of tractors and machinery to bale hay and farm small grains and cover crops. I appreciate the way my parents encouraged my brother and I to embody the work ethic rural life demands while also encouraging us to expand our horizons and pursue our passions. I see now how the farming practices we employed helped to feed people as we did everything we could to care for both the land and the animals that depended on it. Even though I now live in suburban eastern Pennsylvania, I have a strong pull toward that part of my upbringing and take every chance I can to turn over some clay, sow some seeds, and celebrate a healthy harvest.

The property in western Piedmont, North Carolina, has been in the family since the mid-1700s, and it has gone through many changes as successive generations inherited, parceled, and sold various lots along the way. In my lifetime, the number of neighboring farms sold to make subdivisions has changed the landscape drastically. My dad and brother are the last farmers working our family land, and none of us are getting any younger. I wonder and worry sometimes about whether what I remember and value from my childhood will even be around for another generation to experience. My wife and I are unable to have biological children, and in exploring together the way in which we are called to raise and nurture children in our lives, it is natural to think about what we have inherited, and what matters most that we want to pass along. I have a lot I would love to pass on but cannot help thinking that in some ways I am the end of the line.

A. How Would You Like to Be Remembered? A Legacy

This question of legacy is intimately tied to the question of purpose. One cannot honestly answer "how would you like to be remembered?" without concurrently intuiting *What do I want to leave behind when I die?* In our interview process, we began with questions of inspiration, belonging, values, and adversity, and respondents shared their stories. This story-sharing served as a foundation for their reflections on their anticipated legacy. How we anticipate our legacy speaks volumes about how sources of inspiration, belonging, values, and adversity synthesize and shape our current state of being. What do we hope to inspire in others? What kind of space(s) do we wish to create for those whom we encounter along life's journey? What values and wisdom do we hope to pass on to those dependent upon us for care and comfort? How do we learn from our mistakes, struggles, and triumphs so future generations do not have to suffer the same hardship? What vibe do you want to leave behind? Our question, "how do you want to be remembered?" encourages anyone brave enough to venture an answer to integrate these lived experiences, birthing a unique contribution to the cosmos that encompasses yet transcends any singular personal reality.

Each generation uniquely contributes to society and the world they inhabit, and we can see how ideas of legacy evolve in our use of language. Our conceptualization of what we leave behind has shifted dramatically from the generations who used print dictionaries to the ones who browse the internet. Merriam-Webster defines legacy as "(1) a gift by will especially of money or other personal property: BEQUEST; (2) something transmitted by or received from an ancestor or predecessor or from the past."[1] A generic Google search, on the other hand, leads to an article that ponders, "What is a legacy of a person? It is about the richness of the individual's life, including what that person accomplished and the impact he or she had on people and places. Ultimately, the story of a person's life reflects the individual's legacy."[2]

Our conversation partners invite us to consider personal legacies beyond any investments of wealth or property, asking us to focus on the way our treatment of people and places will have a continuing impact. Our relationships and actions during our lifetime communicate our values.

B. On Being Good

Our respondents overwhelmingly expressed the desire to be remembered as "good," with varying degrees of exploration into what being a "good" person means. Our conversation partners spoke in such terms as "someone who contributed in some way," primarily through acts of compassion, accompaniment, and care. The desire to be present for people in times of need, to be remembered as "kind," "always ready to help," "generous," and "a friend to everyone" marks the passions of this group. A sizable number of respondents even said that their anticipated legacy was to be remembered as passionate about something—*anything*—so long as they were able to use their giftedness to be authentic with people, creating space for others to fully express themselves. One conversation partner, *John**, encapsulated these responses with his reflection:

> I want to be remembered as someone who—not even remembered, because I don't want to be famous—but I want my legacy to the people who knew me to be like, "he gave it his all to try to change the world for the better." I don't want my legacy to be one of selfishness, but I want to know, at the point my life is ending, that I really gave my all to try to improve the world from where we found it. I feel like if all of us did that, the world would be a phenomenally better place than it is now.

i. Legacy of Inspiration

In previous chapters, we explored how our conversation partners named their family of origin as a primary source of inspiration. It came as no surprise, then, that they want to be remembered by their own family and closest friends. They connected their anticipated legacy to the influence of their strong family of origin, desiring to pass on the models and values nurtured by their formational caregivers. In anticipating a meaningful legacy, we need to cultivate good networks of family, friends, or colleagues. Conversation partners mentioned those networks by expressing a desire to specifically impact their children, nieces and nephews, and spouses in a positive way.

Our conversation partners valued their family and friend support systems and hoped they would in turn become a positive influence for others. *Maria** shared, "I hope others see me as fearless and courageous, and I want to emulate that because we need more strong women in this world. I also hope that my future children look up to me and I hope that I'm able to raise them to be strong independent adults." Other interviewees expressed a desire to bring joy and laughter to their community and be remembered as someone fun. Above all, our conversation partners shared that they are choosing to be influencers for family and community good.

ii. Legacy of Belonging

The label "influencer" has an extended meaning for someone who uses social media platforms to promote a cause or sell a product. A person receives that label because of the extraordinarily substantial number of "followers" or "listeners" who connect to their social media site. Interestingly, our conversation partners did not share aspirations for becoming social media influencers, instead speaking of the people they interact with face-to-face.

Our conversation partners want to do a good job of being public servants and leave their community a better place through their vocations or community efforts, like teaching children to love to read. They expressed the desire to participate in making the world a better place *together*, highlighting the importance of cultivating belonging. Our conversation partners want to be a part of something, even if that "something" is not a formal organization. As *Emery** said, "I want to be known as someone who didn't just stand by and expect others to step in when things get really tough."

It is noteworthy that few people connected their legacies with their occupations or participation in civic institutions. Except for those in human service vocations, conversation partners focused on the *work* produced in and through these vocations and organizations, *not an attachment to a particular institution.* What mattered most was their desire to encourage and empower people, particularly those in the interviewee's immediate circle, based on common need or shared experience that served as a catalyst for relationship. Many respondents described their legacy as the close communities they helped foster in which the marginalized and disenfranchised felt welcomed, accepted, and nurtured to live authentic lives. A legacy of advocacy and empowerment for the marginalized and the disenfranchised helps solidify a sense of belonging, nurturing that same sense of koinonia for anyone who may be longing for a place to belong.

iii. Legacy of Virtue

Notably missing from our conversation partners' responses were references to passing on fortunes or cementing their names in the annals of history. While there is a great desire to make *some* difference, none of our respondents saw themselves as a potential revolutionary like Dr. Martin Luther King Jr., or a humanitarian, like Mother Teresa. They seemed to have embraced the concept of legacy as the sharing of memorable stories among their close community rather than as monuments of stone or epics regaling them as legendary heroes. *Elias** summed up this shared conviction well:

> I once heard that *good* and *great* are rarely the same man. I used to think I wanted to be remembered as a great man, as a person who did important things, and would have this whole historical legacy. But then I realized it's more about being good to the people around you. Being remembered by people you don't know is not as valuable as being treasured by people who are in your life.

Our conversation partners do not see themselves making their mark in grandiose, trajectory-shifting ways. They showed no desire to be the next fashionista Kim Kardashian, Facebook founder Mark Zuckerberg, entrepreneur Elon Musk, or Amazon billionaire Jeff Bezos. The desire and demand for genuine authenticity and grounded relationships is a testament to the integrity and fortitude with which our conversation partners approach the whole of their lives.

The values distilled from frequently chosen favorite media like *Harry Potter, The Lord of the Rings,* and *Star Wars* are most telling. Harry saves the wizarding world (and by extension, the entire world) with his courage and resistance toward Voldemort—a courage nurtured by a close community of friends and support systems. Frodo only made it to Mt. Doom because of the steadfast devotion of Samwise and the combined efforts of the rest of the fellowship. For all the galaxy-shifting politics in the *Star Wars* saga, it is the arc of small, intimate cells of companionship, struggling against the ongoing efforts of the dark side, that proves to be the triumph of the rebels. Harry, Frodo, and the Skywalkers all come from humble, unassuming origins. Each hopes for a better tomorrow, yet none expects to be cast in the spotlight and to rise as a revolutionary hero. At their best, each returns to the source of their own formation and finds the fortitude to endure. Mercy, accompaniment, and persistence for the greater good expressed in the here and now typify how our conversation partners desire to pass on their own values of the good, be it in a galaxy far, far away, or in the streets and apartments of Anytown, USA.

iv. Legacy and Adversity

Folklore specialist Stith Thompson and mythology specialist Joseph Campbell tell us that the hero journey is a common literary motif in which the would-be hero faces one or multiple difficult tests.[3] If anything, our conversation partners shared the idea that we are all heroes of our own stories in the challenges that life brings us. Inspiration comes because we identify with someone's ability to persevere and the potential for growth in the face of adversity. Necessity forges communities of belonging in the spirit of overcoming systemic injustice to achieve a worthwhile goal, where relationships of solidarity and mutual encouragement overcome life's trials and tribulations. Every good story incorporates at least one adversarial element, and the meaningful pieces of media referenced by our interviewees encapsulate the heroes's journeys, where the protagonists' virtues overcome the vices of evil.

Similarly, conversation partners referenced challenges they were able to overcome. These triumphs contributed to their anticipated legacies. Those who felt ostracized because of their race, sexual orientation, or gender identity were committed to cultivating communities of belonging where the virtues of equity, acceptance, and reconciliation served as an inspiration for others who have endured similar prejudice. Interviewees who are also parents recalled memories of a difficult childhood due to abuse, neglect, or economic hardship, and committed themselves to leaving a legacy that ensures that their own children would not continue the destructive cycle. Others shared experiences with mental health crises, and the desire to accompany others through various treatments and therapies so that a fuller, more joyful existence might blossom. Underpinning the desire to be good is the courage, persistence, and resiliency to face adverse situations and to come through them as stronger people.

C. Good 'nough?

Psychologists Jean Twenge and William Campbell have critiqued the generations spanning our conversation partners' demographics, citing an increase in narcissistic behavior and diagnosed narcissistic personality disorder (NPD) as a moral failure in our cultural makeup.[4] Their book, *The Narcissism Epidemic*, posits that poor parenting techniques geared toward raising a child's self-esteem have created generations of self-absorbed, entitled, fame-seeking socialites who do not express genuine, altruistic care toward others without some level of self-gratification.[5] Our preoccupation with social media may lead to an obsession in creating the perfect public image rather than developing face-to-face relationships. Narcissists would rather seek individual glory than work as a team.

Our question of legacy produced an entirely different insight into the lives of our conversation partners. While Twenge and Campbell showed an increase in narcissistic traits in emerging generations, we did not hear this in our interviews. Responses ranging from "I don't care if I'm remembered at all" to "I want to make a difference for just one person" do not contain the self-absorption which

The Narcissism Epidemic illustrates. While even the notion of considering one's legacy may seem narcissistic, our

Our respondents demonstrated a genuine altruism founded on deep convictions of empathy, care, and justice for the sake of others, not entitled self-interest.

respondents demonstrated a genuine altruism founded on deep convictions of empathy, care, and justice for the sake of others, not entitled self-interest.

Our conversation partners are deeply concerned for the well-being of others, expressing in conversation how their careers in social services, public advocacy, and matters of environmental and social justice stem from this concern. Their reasoning is *not* because it makes them feel good about themselves. Rather, they indicated that our shared human legacy is worthy of investment in a genuine conviction that all people share the responsibility to nurture the lives of others.

D. "Goodness/Kindness" and Biblical Heritage

Jesus once told a story in which a man is robbed, beaten, and left dying on the roadside. Two religious leaders saw the man and chose to pass by and continue their journey. In Jesus's story, told to a mixed community of Jews and Samaritans, a man from Samaria had stopped and rescued the man, ensuring he would fully recover. There were cultural differences and animosity between these two groups of people. Jesus meant to challenge the assumptions of the listeners. Jesus asked his audience, "Now which of the three would you say was a neighbor to the man who was attacked by bandits?" to which they replied, "The one who showed him mercy."[6]

Even if people have never heard the biblical story of the Good Samaritan, its influence permeates our culture. People understand that "Good Samaritan" refers to someone who comes to another person's aid, even at a cost to themselves. Fred Rogers, a television host and Presbyterian minister, taught generations of children the value of being a kind and generous "neighbor" to those around us. He filled children's lives with examples of living by the "Golden Rule" of treating others as you wish to be treated. Superheroes of the comics and movies are popular because they have the power to rescue people from harm and to defend ordinary people from the designs of sinister characters.

As the Good Samaritan story fades from the American population's repertoire, we are in danger of losing the wider concept of who our neighbors are. In stories from *Harry Potter, Star Wars,* or the Marvel Cinematic Universe, which have replaced those like the Good Samaritan in the popular well of common cultural references, the notion of neighbor is not encountered on a one-to-one parallel. Protagonists showing mercy to the oppressed and afflicted are people equipped with powers of magic, the Force, or genetic and experimental enhancements that set them apart from the recipients of aid. The capacity to offer relief is at an imbalance compared to that of the Samaritan, who is depicted as a normal traveler with no superpowers. What's more, Harry Potter, Luke Skywalker, and Spider-Man are all *protagonists*, set up from the beginning of their stories to be emerging (if not reluctant) heroes who rise above and save the day. The Samaritan traveler is actually at a considerable disadvantage, since the people hearing this story from Jesus would view a Samaritan as an enemy, outsider, and pariah. For this Samaritan to offer mercy requires something more than an obligation to employ their powers responsibly. Mercy in the character of the Samaritan requires vulnerability, personal sacrifice, and the willingness to redefine the way we are perceived and encountered by people who receive us as enemies. The dynamic is entirely different, necessitating, as our conversation partners expressed through their perceived legacy, a renewed engagement with what it means to be a neighbor in the twenty-first century.

Arianna* shared that she wanted to be remembered as "a person who was kind to everyone. It doesn't matter who they were, where they came from, or what their story was. That I was nonjudgmental and open to them for who they were and helped where I could." Being nonjudgmental and respecting all people without exception embodies the character of being a good neighbor to "others" who are not part of our inner circle. In this way, "enemies" become friends with whom we have yet to make an acquaintance.

E. All We Have Is Now: Living Memories and Enduring Stories

i. Personal Legacies

A legacy consists not only in the works produced by the lives of the deceased, but also in the memory of their impact inherited through the process of storytelling. As Ursula K. Le Guin puts it in The Tombs of Atuan: "Most things grow old and perish, as the centuries go on and on. Very few are the precious things that remain precious, or the tales that are still told."[7] What remains of our memories after we die throughout the passage of time? Will we be remembered, and by whom? What stories will people tell of us when we have died? Those who study oral history or family traditions have noted that most people are remembered for two or three generations after they die. Siblings and their children will share eyewitness accounts of the deceased person, which may be remembered and retold for one or two more generations before they are forgotten. Surprisingly, a considerable number of respondents did not have any strong convictions about how they wanted to be remembered. Nevaeh* told us:

I don't care to be remembered at all. It's not important to me. Once I'm dead, I'm dead. That's it. I hope that while I'm alive people consider me as someone they can go to for help and support, who won't judge them. That's what I care about. *I care about my time here because I believe it's what I have.* [emphasis added]

While there is great power in thinking about how one's life will endure beyond our mortal existence, there is also great responsibility in recognizing that sometimes we tend to approach that question with a faulty self-perception. We repeatedly heard something similar from respondents: They do not care about what kind of legacy they leave behind. We found that many had not thought about their legacy and were working out their thoughts during the interview. Some were able to identify what they hoped to leave behind and others struggled to come to a conclusion. A few responded to the implied religious question of "beyond this life" and indicated their view is that "dead means done." This is not to say, however, that these interviewees have a *laissez-faire* attitude about their place in the world. Taking the scope of their interviews into consideration, these respondents seemed to say that to think about their own legacy is to build themselves up into something they are not. "I won't care when I'm dead" speaks to the notion that life is best lived for the here and now, because when death comes, there will be no do-over. It is not up to us to theorize about what kind of impact we might leave on the world, but to engage the world while there is still time to do so.

These words from our partners echo the words of the teacher in the Old Testament book of Ecclesiastes:

Both [All] go to the same place—they came from dust and they return to dust... So I saw that there is nothing better for people than to be happy in their work. That is our lot in life. And *no one can bring us back to see what happens after we die.*[8] [emphasis added]

Death comes for all, and yet it remains an unknowable mystery. Ecclesiastes 3 echoes this sentiment from our conversation partners, who insisted that to "enjoy the work" is the ultimate reward. We cannot take it with us when we are dead.

ii. Communal Legacy

We are corporate beings, persons in community whose legacy extends beyond a personal sphere of influence into our society. What we did not hear from our conversation partners were plans to create or maintain *institutions* through which a legacy of goodness would perpetuate. We have already spoken to the recognition that there is no desire to bolster institutional mechanisms for the sake of organizational security. Emerging generations are more likely to change jobs rather than develop loyalty to a company, which may or may not be around to offer a pension upon retirement. They grew up hearing of corporations that chose profit over safe environmental practices and of religious and nonprofit organizational leaders embroiled in financial or sexual scandals.

On the other hand, emerging generations will donate generously and seemingly spontaneously to GoFundMe causes rather than making regular bank transfers to organizations that have traditionally offered aid and assistance to those in need. Faith communities that have relied on institutional security to keep the legacy of the faith tradition alive in successive generations are experiencing this shift firsthand as a challenge to their survival. Service and civic organizations, social clubs, and religious communities have an opportunity to embody the potential for a robust communal legacy by focusing on their societal impact and enrichment, rather than on the personal benefit to member donors.

Communities have practices that serve as legacy. Take, for instance, the notion of "paying it forward," an expression used among our respondents. This concept became popular through the 2000 movie of the same title, which was loosely based on a novel about a young boy who completes a school assignment to do something to make the world a better place. The boy decides to do three kind things for three people, urging them each to pay the kindness forward to three others. In this way, kindness expands exponentially. Paying it forward has turned into a movement, such as paying for the meal of someone behind you at the drive through. Incidences captured on social media encourage others to "pay it forward" rather than "pay it back," as with a loan. This movement may describe a vehicle for fostering communal legacy that engages emerging generations for whom transformative experiences are more important than institutional security or personal status in the face of our uncertain future.

F. That-Which-Shall-Not-Be-Named

Death.

In Western culture, death has been both glorified in various forms of consumable media and sterilized in the way we approach and talk about it (if we talk about it at all). Pets "cross over the rainbow bridge," and loved ones "pass away," because even to say that a person "died" seems to acquiesce to an unseen and indomitable power. We invest billions each year to prolong life at all costs, sacrificing quality of life to fend off the reaper and maintain our place of existence. Davey Jones's intimidating question, "Do you fear death?" receives a resounding "Yes!" in our culture, even among people who insist that religious convictions protect from fearing the valley of death's dark shadow.

Despite carrying out these interviews during the Covid-19 pandemic, it was intriguing to note that few, if any, of our conversation partners referred to the massive death toll. In the first weeks of Covid, national news outlets flooded airwaves with images of over-capacity morgues and bolded death counts filling screens with startling intensity. Those images and statistics rapidly transformed to a B-roll of barren shelves where toilet paper once filled the aisle, interviews about the mask mandate debate, and frenzied commentary about the state of our national economy if prolonged lockdown should continue. The data on Covid transmission rates and death tolls became relegated to a scroll at the bottom of the screen, like school closures on a snow day or "scores around the league" during a football game. They were there for you to find them, but only for those deeply invested in their findings.

Reflecting this trend, our conversation partners spoke about the need to adjust vocational obligations during quarantine, the struggle of balancing childcare with graduate school, and the necessity to reevaluate and reprioritize life in the face of routine upheaval. The opportunity to begin (and now, continue) working from home rather than reporting to an office, and the leisure of attending school from a comfy chair in sweats with a midday margarita in their mug received notable praise. Elsewhere, lament over the inability to gather in person at school or at places of worship escalated, encouraging people to not hide their smiles or to gather without fear as a testament to a strong faith. The conversation around Covid shifted more toward its inconveniencing of our "normal lives," rather than its impact as a global health crisis that consumes life in death. Across all of the questions from our interview exchanges that occurred in early 2021, only one respondent referred to a Covid-related death. Instead, respondents talked about the effects of Covid on work–life balance, childcare, and personal networking opportunities and social interactions. Missing in this avoidance of death was the ability to recognize the largest problem presented by Covid: People die, and we have little to no agency against such an adversary.

As clergy working closely with the process of death and burial, we recognize the increase in bereaved

> **Missing in this avoidance of death was the ability to recognize the largest problem presented by Covid: People die, and we have little to no agency against such an adversary.**

families. Two area funeral directors shared with us that their census of such families increased by 150 percent, even a full year after vaccines became publicly available.[9] Peaks and valleys in the infection rate caused periods of brief respite and extreme taxation on this system of healthcare workers, funeral providers, grief support programs, chaplains, and religious consolation ministries. Yet in the mainstream, a relatively brief time passed before the trauma of pandemic-related death gave way to the numbness of isolation-induced boredom. Even in the Christian tradition, which has at the core of its belief system a story of the cycle of death and resurrection, death remains something that occurs at the end of *a* life, rather than a systemic plague that destroys *all* life.

Our bodies are not the only things to die, and Covid serves as a reminder of the seeming totality of death. Relationships die as people grow apart or experience a divorce or breakup. Organizations die when the lifeblood of purpose dries up and members stop investing resources to maintain a common mission. Our environment is steadily experiencing death as greenhouse gases continue to rise while corporate waste pollutes rivers, streams, and ecosystems vital to planetary survival. In our shared experience, death is "that-which-shall-not-be-named," because of the fear, discomfort, pain, grief, and uncertainty associated with the harsh reality of mortality. It's safe to say, then, that we cannot anticipate a personal or communal legacy if we refuse to even consider death.

Acknowledging the reality of death is a first step toward cultivating communities where personal and corporate legacy can produce the transformative experience necessary for successive generations to thrive. Rituals can nurture healthy acknowledgement of mortality and equip persons in community to endure life's greatest adversary, as we receive inspiration from the past, experience belonging in the present, and instill values persistent beyond death.

G. Death, Ritual, and Remembrance

In moments of death, we come together to bury the dead, share memories of the deceased, and honor their memory by creating a legacy of our own. Some believe that ancient cultures formulated belief systems to answer the one unanswerable question, *What happens after we die?* All people, regardless of their religious affiliation, or lack thereof, experience the reality of death and the grief that accompanies it, necessitating a communal ritual that allows people to enter into the mystery of this question and process its meaning in their own lives.

i. Death and Ritual

The ritual of death is participatory. Commonly, when we think of death rituals, we are referring to funerals (with some form of bodily remains present) or memorials (no bodily remains present). Viewings (a time to meet the family and view the deceased's body in the casket) or wakes (gatherings after a funeral service where mourners console one another and tell stories about the deceased) serve as opportunities for loved ones to gather either before or after a formal service. Often, family and friends will organize or participate in a charity walk or marathon if their loved one suffered from a chronic disease like cancer, Alzheimer's, or multiple sclerosis, to reference a few. Eulogies, photo collages, the scattering of ashes, planting a tree, or visiting favorite hangouts of the deceased serve as common ways people pay their respects to the dead. Mourners erect thoughtfully spontaneous memorials at the site of mass casualties, like the rows of pictures, candles, and stuffed animals that lined fences outside of Robb Elementary School in Ulvalde, Texas, following a mass shooting in spring of 2022. Roadside memorials mark the sites of car accidents, and window decals or bumper stickers pay tribute to loved ones. Fraternal organizations have created rituals to honor the service of their former members in death.

Another way family members ritualize death is through advocacy. When a loved one dies through an act of violence, trauma, addiction, or by suicide, advocacy work for supportive legislation is a way to ritualize their experience toward healing, promote awareness, and effect change for others facing similar circumstances. Each of these examples points to the expansive and evolving nature of ritualizing the death of a loved one. These rituals might not incorporate a religious service, and yet they hold deep meaning and allow healing to begin for those who are grieving.

Reflecting on their anticipated legacy, our conversation partners expressed a somberly optimistic reflection on the rituals associated with death. *Krista* recalled her grandfather's funeral and celebrated how his coworkers at the police department and other members of the community were in attendance to show their support to the family and to witness the impact of his life. "They just had the nicest things to say about him, so that... got me thinking I... hope that people would have the same things to say about me, that I was helpful, someone to go to, whether it was for advice, friendship."

Violet recalled:

I used to want to be kind of well-known and famous, I
think very American, someone well-known and famous
and remarkable in some way, shape, or form. And now
when I think about my, you know, what will be said at my
funeral, I want the narrative to be "she heard me, and she
challenged me."

Kennedy* expressed "I want my funeral to have hundreds and
hundreds of people from throughout my life who I've touched,
who I've helped, and who know that I've always been authentic. I
like to give back, and we are nothing without our community and
charity."

From another perspective, on discovering the death of a
friend trending on social media, *Ed** commented "I don't want
to be remembered publicly,... because that's pretty traumatic [for
me]," choosing instead to focus on how close family members,
chosen family, and close friends would be the preferred community of remembrance.

From large occasions where the entire community rallies to
support one another by remembering the deceased, to intimate
gatherings of loved ones to celebrate the life of their loved one, the
common theme is for the ritual to offer condolence, comfort, and
community in the wake of death's isolating rift. Sharing stories of
remembrance edifies those gathered to provide mutual support in
moments of grief, depression, isolation, and uncertainty. *Genesis**
encapsulated this theme with her memories of joining her parents
to visit the gravesites of family members, celebrating that "this is
the family cemetery where everyone's buried forever, and you can
go back all the generations. We're a storytelling family, so we tell
stories." Capitalizing on the opportunity to keep the story going
is key to how our interviewees experience death rituals. This can
also serve as a point of connection with religious communities of
varied faith traditions, which utilize rituals of death to perpetuate

the story of a shared faith alongside the stories of personal enrichment and hope.

ii. Death and Remembrance

Our conversation partners do not worry about what happens to their physical bodies after death when it comes to death rituals. Rather, their primary concern is what happens to the people who love them, and whom they love, after they're gone. In her response, *Skylar** candidly shared:

> **I do not give a single shit about how I'm remembered. I want to be remembered in a way that's going to help my friends and family grieve properly, so whatever they need to do to heal and grow after I die, that's all I really care about. I don't necessarily care if I have a legacy, I don't care—like, I'll be dead, so what does it matter?**
>
> **—Skylar***

I do not give a single shit about how I'm remembered. I want to be remembered in a way that's going to help my friends and family grieve properly, so whatever they need to do to heal and grow after I die, that's all I really care about. I don't necessarily care if I have a legacy, I don't care—like, I'll be dead, so what does it matter?

What we are finding, however, is that emerging generations have no clue where to look for support in this endeavor, in large part due to disenfranchisement from faith communities. The tragic irony in this is that faith communities have practices of offering communal support in moments of tragedy and grief integrated into their cultural DNA. The strong desire to provide opportunities for their loved ones to grieve in a healthy, expressive way is because their own experiences with death have not afforded them the resources to process the raw emotions that emerge during the most debilitating moments of life.

Jesus understood death and so did his earliest followers. In the Christian tradition, Jesus spoke often of his own death even as he offered his closest friends hope in life after death. The signature stories of the Christian faith are the stories of Jesus's death and resurrection, which followers retell, reenact, and celebrate each year at Easter as a reminder of hope and new life. The cross is a symbol and instrument of death, and Christians use this symbol as an object of remembrance and hope. It points toward a legacy of remembrance.

Pointing to the necessity of communal rituals that emphasize care, Ray S. Anderson's work *Spiritual Caregiving as Secular Sacrament* offers a robust synthesis of the rituals of faith communities with the life experiences of our shared humanity.[10] Anderson defines *sacrament* as a mediation of spirituality in the encounter of humans with each other.[11] In sharing physical, emotional, or rational relationships with others, we engage the body's needs for health, stimulation, and nurture. However, without the expression of care, these relationships are essentially transactional, and lack the spiritual component that unites persons beyond physical, emotional, or rational space. The mediation of care between humans is inherently spiritual, whether physical, social, emotional, or psychological. For Anderson, all caregiving is spiritual caregiving and is not an exclusively religious exercise. What is important is that this mediation of spiritual caregiving is an ongoing exchange among members of a community, centered around a commonly held ritual that binds people together beyond personal need.

The legacy of faith traditions persists in the sacred stories and rituals communities celebrate in shared practice. Casper ter Kuile describes four levels of ritual: connecting with self, connecting with others, connecting with nature, and connecting with transcendence. He draws heavily on the wisdom and practices of faith traditions for his suggestions of ritual at each level. These practices have ancient roots and have been reimagined and repackaged as one generation passes them to the next. Every society has traditions for sharing meals. Jewish communities celebrate the Seder meal to commemorate their history as God's people. The Islamic annual tradition of Ramadan ends in a grand feast, Eid al-Fitr. Americans and Canadians mark national holidays of Thanksgiving centered around gathering for a wonderful meal. Accompanying these feasts are rituals of prayers, blessings, and the retelling of stories that unite the participants in shared experiences.

iii. Ritual and Remembrance

Within Christian faith communities, the two primary rituals of baptism and communion serve as opportunities to mediate care and are intrinsically linked to the act of remembrance, ritualization of death, and healing for the gathered community. Christians receive baptism as a burial with Jesus in death and are raised with him into the promise of resurrection life (Romans 6:1–11). In this rite, the imagery of death and rebirth is central to communicating a transcendent reality of deep belonging, concurrently teaching the values and modeling the character of communal life. Tied to our conversations from chapters 2 and 3, baptism also incorporates rituals of belonging, values, and legacy with the images of life and death, because these are things that connect us all as humans.

On the night before his execution, Jesus celebrated what the synoptic Gospels describe as the Jewish Passover meal with his closest friends and followers. Interpreting this sacred ritual in view of his impending death, Jesus shared this meal so that they would remember him and have something to carry on once he is no longer present among them. Christians of a variety of expressions continue to participate in this ritual of remembrance and presence, trusting that it satisfies and nurtures Jesus's present-day followers as we face our own mortality experienced in the grief of this world's turmoil. In sharing this ritual, we know that God continues to be present among us, even on the brink of death. The core of the message and the practice of the ritual remain the same; we participate in this ritual to remember Jesus, in whom all are remembered as people loved and cherished by a generous God. We cannot ignore, however, that this ritual is intimately tied to the reality of death and persists as an act of remembrance that evokes the paradox of mortality.[12]

At its best, this ritual creates a space where people are fed, the senses are engaged, and mechanical repetition gives way to authentic personhood in communal sharing. Faith communities have often lost the ability to allow these and other rituals to evoke the imagination, so that the Lord's Supper is no longer a legacy proclaimed for others, but something absorbed solely for personal gratification and entitlement.

Through these examples of religious ritual, we see that a legacy does not remain with the one in whom it originates, but it passes on to those who receive and celebrate it. What we do is not about self-edification or memorialization; it is about sharing ritual space for the communal enrichment of those gathered in anticipation of those who come after. Like funerals, wakes, charity walks, and End of Watch calls, the rituals associated with death are meant to serve as vehicle for mediating care among mourners, expressed toward the person or people whose care nurtured them in life. Additionally, offering these rituals as an extension of care beyond the boundaries of Christian community can provide an opportunity for others to experience the elements of curiosity, mystery, and wonder that commingle with the throes of grief in an environment where people at different stages of their own grief journey can accompany one another in authentic expressions of care.

Because all people experience the reality of death and grief, all people are situated somewhere in the cycle of grief, otherwise known by its five stages: denial, anger, bargaining, depression, and acceptance. Those of us in Co.lab.inq who are clergy encounter families from among our own faith communities and the neighborhoods where we serve who grieve with expressions too painful for words, in part because their deceased loved one wished to have no communal gathering upon their death. No funeral, no memorial, no celebration of life. No opportunity for people to share how much this person meant to them, what their contributions to this world mean for those who received them, and how much they will be missed. People of faith can use their gifts for ritualizing death, memorializing loved ones, and encountering grief in a healthy, expressive manner as a service to those who endure pain and suffering in the lonely chasm caused by the gloom of death and dying.

Concurrently, the legacy our conversation partners articulated most clearly is the legacy of intentional, genuine, radical care, transcending boundaries and barriers established by the systems and schemata of our segmented social groupings for the sake of a better world. The desire to be good is essentially the desire to embody care. Moving forward, religious communities and nones and dones can cocreate spaces where rituals are untethered from institutional barriers and embraced as a legacy of imagination, wonder, and authentic personhood in shared community for the sake of radical, holistic care.

H. Cocreating Ritual Space

One component of ritual participation often involves the recognition of a shared space where generations gather to practice the traditions they inherited from previous practitioners. The allure of places like Lambeau Field, Broadway, Yankee Stadium, or other noteworthy venues captivate because within them there exists a liminal suspension of time, where people gather to participate in the culture associated with a game or a show. These grand spaces reflect more intimate ones, like the home passed down through generations of a family lineage or a worship space marked with the memory of generations of gatherers. In our rapidly changing world, families are not passing the farm down from generation to generation. Church buildings and campuses are no longer communal centers. Yet the need for these spaces exists as far as emerging generations long for interaction with people in an intimate, formative experience.

In an environment where statistics report the rapid closure of mainline Protestant, Catholic, Orthodox, Jewish, and Muslim communities of faith in the United States, what legacy do they leave? Quite often, the questions communities ask are: *Where have all the young people gone? Will this place still be around when I die, so that I can be buried out of this building where I was married, buried my spouse, and forged relationships with lifelong friends? Have we failed our parents, who built these places of worship with their own blood, sweat, and calloused hands? What will remain to pass on to our children, our grandchildren, if this community of faith dies? Are we the end of the line?*

Economists Stuart Butler and Carmen Diaz describe Americans as spending much of their time in first and second spaces (homes and workplaces, respectively).[13] Drawing on an idea pioneered by sociologist Ray Oldenburg, urban planners are recognizing a need for creating "third places" where people can routinely and easily connect with others. From the perspective of urban development, parks, recreational centers, coffee shops, co-ops, hair salons, and spas serve as necessary components of urban planning for creating third places.[14] These third places are environments where relationship-building can occur in a fluid exchange of personhood as people exercise, refresh themselves, and connect with others outside their normal sphere of influence.

Our conversation partners described third spaces as non-physical environments where people's needs are met without being tied to a specific location. Venues for recreation, performing arts, and exercise for their bodies and imaginations are necessary, but non-static. What matters most is the creation of a "space" where passions can develop, and rituals can be celebrated as enrichment for all involved; where equity and mutual participation in life transcends socioeconomic barriers, ethno-religious identifiers, social hierarchies, and common affiliation with a particular locale.

Conversation partners described third spaces as nonphysical environments where people's needs are met without being tied to a specific location.

In previous generations, faith community structures thrived as hubs for third spaces that provided ritual space. In northeast Pennsylvania, parents' groups, youth leagues, garden clubs, community dinners, and social outreach initiatives found their support localized in the efforts of those unified by a particular faith tradition, particularly Christian churches. Our conversation partners articulated that, in their experience, such institutions no longer support an environment of imagination and wonder engaging in accessible ritual. Rather, faith communities are fending off the fear of institutional death by bolstering the physical spaces they occupy, turning the ritual space of communal enrichment into an ornate mausoleum of the walking dead. Religious convictions are no doubt present to inspire and encourage communities to cultivate belonging and instill inherited values in the face of our world's numerous adversities. Passover, Ramadan, and eucharistic meals still incorporate ritual practices. Nones and dones, however, have experienced these and other rituals from faith communities as void of substance beyond the moment of physical engagement, not transforming the behavior of adherents beyond the act of worship. Integrating religious beliefs authentically with lived practices to create space for others to participate in nurturing rituals is essential to turning physical third spaces into ritual spaces of communal enrichment.

Consider how convictions of environmentalism and creation care held within faith traditions might be reimagined as a physical legacy for successive generations contributed to by the religiously unaffiliated. Creating community gardens to alleviate food insecurity goes hand in hand with taking a hike to enjoy the beauty of the mountainside for personal meditation. In this way, a third space becomes a ritual space, where the good of the environment benefits the creatures that depend on it for survival and place aesthetic value on our planet's natural biodiversity. Like the Greek proverb ponders, "Blessed are they who plant a tree under whose shade they will never sit." Communities that are thriving seem to be authentically investing their energies into cocreating ritual spaces with both members and nonmembers for the sake of the larger neighborhoods, with the third space fluidly transitioning to the parks, shelters, schools, and shops that surround the worship facilities.

I. Summary

Does my life contribute to something I would be willing to claim after I am dead? Was it good? Did it mean anything? Our conversation partners taught us that there is a deep desire to be a part of something to which they can direct their passion in a way that authentically reflects their core values. This generation expresses a self-perception that they are making their mark in a small, localized place. There is a general conviction that the world is never going to change. People will be people. Racism, sexism, economic disparity, environmental catastrophe—these things will always be here. It won't change. And yet, it definitely won't change so long as we stay still, remain silent, and refuse to be the change we want to see in the world.

In this, we see that nones and dones from emerging generations and people deeply enmeshed in the active lives of faith communities have much more in common—and much more for which to strive together—than we often realize. If we can articulate our anticipated legacy in a way that encompasses our formational sources of inspiration, belonging, values, and adversity, then we can move forward together, positioning ourselves to engage in the process of building ritual spaces that produce valuable legacies that will outlast any of us.

Take a note from our conversation partners. Pay attention to the places where our personal and communal hopes for an anticipated legacy are irrelevant when compared to the immense potential for improving the lives of others purely for their benefit.

Consider the kind of legacy we are maintaining with the intent of passing it on to others. Are we sure that the legacy we are leaving is of value to those who will inherit it? Passing off Great-Great-Grandma's silver tea set may be important to you because you inherited it from your parents. What if it is not what our children want or need? What if we have lost the family story that goes with it? How can a legacy allow the next generation to thrive and create rituals of their own to pass on?

Anticipating a meaningful legacy requires intentionality. Encourage the hard conversations, even if it is uncomfortable to think about a time after your death or to imagine a not-yet-lived reality. The question of legacy demands to be asked, because if we have learned anything throughout this entire process, a legacy is not about *me*, it is about *us*.

Even though we may not understand what happens after we die, maintaining our legacy requires us to move forward with hope. Our rituals of care and spirituality help us embody hope for self and neighbor. Care deeply. Inspire others. Build communities of belonging. Internalize, imitate, and influence virtuous values. Overcome and abolish adversity. Leave a legacy that endures. Create good vibes.

J. For Further Group Discussion

1. How would you like to be remembered? Personally? As a family? As a community?

2. How do you feel about death? Is there anything you fear about death? Why do we find it so hard to talk about death?

3. How has reading this chapter shaped your thoughts around your own legacy?

4. Cultural definitions of "legacy" have shifted over time. What might "legacy" mean for coming generations? How might we participate in birthing that for future generations?

5. What is the most important thing you want to hand over to someone else? Why?

6. What happens when you inherit a legacy that you do not feel responsible for maintaining?

7. Compare the Good Samaritan story (Luke 10:30–37) with *Harry Potter*, *Star Wars*, and Spider-Man. How are the characters the same? How are they different? What stories will communicate our shared values with the next generation?

8. Fred Rogers's Lifetime Achievement Award acceptance speech[15] invited people to take 10 seconds to reflect upon a person who impacted their lives and shaped their being. Take time to do the same and share with others how that influences you today.

9. Fred Rogers also modelled cocreating ritual space in his "neighborhood" using television. How has the global pandemic experience enabled you to cocreate ritual space using media such as Zoom and Instagram?

10. Paying it forward is a positive concept to help us think outside our own needs and desires. What opportunities do you see in your sphere of influence to pay it forward, and contribute to a legacy of good?

REFRAMING
THE UNFRAMABLE

Stephen Simmons & Jill Peters, Authors
Bonnie Bates, Editor

"There was never really a design for, a design for love, I think."
—*Larry**

But Moses said to God, "If I now come to the Israelites and say to them, 'The God of your ancestors has sent me to you,' they are going to ask me, 'What is this God's name?' What am I supposed to say to them?" God said to Moses, "I Am Who I Am."
—Exodus 3:13–14

"As we are always leaking reverence, so we must always look for new ways to replenish it."
—Paul Woodruff[1]

JANET'S STORY

As a young adult, I joined the Peace Corps and was sent to the Fiji Islands. I was eager for adventure, but I also harbored this idea of finding out if the faith I had grown up with was strictly suited for Americans or if people of other cultures and backgrounds had something to teach me about spirituality or a life of faith. I lived with a Fijian family in a remote village. On Sundays, we attended church with most of the village. I remember being astonished that I knew exactly what was going on during the service even though I didn't understand the language. There was no sign of the loose-fitting colorful clothes the villagers wore the rest of the week; everyone was in black and white. The tunes of all the hymns were recognizable, and I knew exactly when they were answering the call to worship, confessing and being assured of being pardoned, reciting the Lord's Prayer, and hearing the benediction. And from the Bible reading I was pretty sure I knew the sermon was a stern admonition to be obedient. You might think that I was comforted by the familiarity of the entire service, but the opposite was true. "The faith" had been transplanted, but it hadn't taken root in native soil. I was disappointed that there were few elements of the Fijian culture as part of the service, and I wondered if there was more to their faith than the rules and rituals passed onto them. I spent the next two years exploring the animistic faith of the Fijian people and the Hindu faith of the Fijian Indian people. As I listened to the stories of these other religions and experienced some of their practices, I realized that the Bible stories were amazingly rich and full of grace for everyone. Those years helped me to decide to join the work of Bible translation. I had come to understand the Bible as a treasure, and I wanted others to be able to read or hear the words for themselves and to allow those words to impact their lives.

AIDEN'S* STORY

What I grew up in was basically "Here's the truth (i.e., the Bible) now make everything about you and the world fit into this framework." Whereas where I am today, where a lot of inner work has taken me is to an understanding that if we're doing the work that's required, we can trust ourselves ultimately and trust our inner experience that we don't have to have it figured out. And the system I grew up in was all about belief, and I—where I am today—is much more about finding solidarity in community, being open to experiences of beauty and mystery and wonder and experiencing God in that way, but not really feeling. For instance, if you asked me "What do you believe?" I would probably say that I don't find that to be a relevant question at this stage because I can tell you what I've experienced. To me, that's much more relevant than what I believe. So yeah, that's my answer to that.

DEBBIE'S* STORY

With tapes [referring to duplicated VHS or cassette tapes], every time you make a copy of a copy, they called it losing a generation, so you would lose some of the quality, right? So... if we keep trying to do the same thing with the church and trying to make a copy of a copy of a copy, we're going to lose an entire generation.

A. Just Do Good

The question that heads this chapter had not been in our original plan, but shortly after we began the interview process, our interviewees wondered, "Why haven't you asked, 'How have your beliefs changed?'" We explained that we had not wanted to make our interviews overly "churchy," but to keep them more neutral in a religious sense. As we discovered, and as other studies have borne

> **They didn't so much break with the church as drift away from it. They simply found no compelling reason to stay.**

out, relatively few of our conversation partners were militant atheists or agnostics. More than a few said that they have a close relationship with God, pray regularly, read the Bible, and engage in other spiritual practices, but feel no need to be part of a faith community. On the whole, our conversation partners were most likely to fit the category of "nothing in particular." Many of them had grown up in church and expressed gratitude for the values and sense of community they had found there and wanted to pass on to their children. However, over time, work and family obligations, and the fact that Sunday was often their only time to kick back and regroup (a kind of secular Sabbath, so to speak), had caused them not so much to break with the church as to drift away from it. They simply found no compelling reason to stay.

> My dad was Greek Orthodox, my mom was Jewish. We celebrated the holidays in that we had a menorah and a Christmas tree, but we never went into the meaning behind any of it... And so I never really grew up with religion... I just kind of wrote it off, and simply didn't think much of it or that it has much value. But that aside, over the years since then I think there's so much good messaging in faith and religion that anybody can learn from... I would say that even though I don't have any real formal religion or faith or belief in God, I still see so much value in connecting with one another, right? Like we can still all be striving for the same things, we can all still be connected and trying to do good in the world...
>
> —Heather*

> I don't think that I'm lacking in faith; I just don't feel a need, or I don't think it does anything for me to go to church. I do wonder about the girls sometimes. We're not raising them to *not* believe in God, we just don't actively participate in anything well.
>
> —Dennis*

> While I will always believe that religion can be super-helpful for most people, it doesn't really speak to me any longer.
>
> —Jack*

Many of those who had been raised in a church were now religious entrepreneurs who sampled from a variety of faith traditions, including various forms of nature religion like Wicca. Others spoke of finding a path at this point in their lives that fit them based on their personality type. They understood that their participation might well change in the future. They hadn't so much drifted away as circulated among various religious affiliations. The idea of practicing a specific discipline over time didn't have much traction—with the occasional exception of yoga—while the language of "being on a journey" was very prominent.

Many of those who had been raised in a church were now religious entrepreneurs who sampled from a variety of faith traditions.

*Liam**, who had remained loosely within the Christian orbit, put it this way:

> I think I've always been a little bit of a chameleon Christian who doesn't find a lot of reasons to be put off by a whole lot of Christian environments. And really the question for me tends to be what the focus is in each new space, and what's the focus for me in my particular timeline. Is it service, is it helping people, is it just being with and helping through their own life journey as a community, is it raising my kids? You know, what does it look like?

On the other hand, quite a few could say with some precision why and when they had turned their backs on the church, and often on Christianity as such. Some mentioned clergy abuse, not only in the abstract, but also in their own personal experience. A number reported having suffered various forms of emotional trauma from congregations of which they had been a part.

A few felt that the church had become too enmeshed in politics. For many, the watershed moment had come during college, often in comparative religion classes or courses in which they were encouraged to take a critical stance toward the Bible. Typically, nothing in their prior church experience had prepared them for this. Many people made comments like the following:

> I think where I landed is just like living in the space of mystery where I think that there's truth in all the great religions, beautiful lessons we can learn in how to live a good life, a meaningful life, but I don't ascribe to any particular one, and I think I sort of trust that there are forces greater than us and I don't know what they are. I don't necessarily call it "the universe" or "love" or "mystery," right?
>
> —Tiana*

One of our respondents' biggest turn-offs about the church was their perception that it claimed to have exclusive "secret" knowledge that was not open to discussion (this is hardly a new complaint!). Often enough, when they had asked perfectly reasonable questions, they were told not to question, but simply to accept and obey, without further explanation. The irony here, of course, is that it was precisely the practitioners of mystery religions and gnostic sects who claimed to have this kind of secret knowledge, and whom Jesus and the early church repudiated. The gospel was, on the contrary, an "open secret" to those willing to receive it with ready hearts: "At that time Jesus said, 'I thank you, Father, Lord of heaven and earth, because you have hidden these things from the wise and the intelligent and have revealed them to infants.'" (Mt. 11:25, NRSVue)

Along the same lines, speaking to the church in Corinth, Paul said, "Consider your own call, brothers and sisters: not many

of you were wise by human standards, not many were powerful, not many were of noble birth. But God chose what is fool-
ish in the world to shame the wise" (1 Cor 1:26–27a, NRSVue).
He addressed some of his most pointed criticism to those "super
Christians" who claimed that their extraordinary spiritual gifts
put them a cut above everyone else. In fact, famously comparing the church to the human body, he went so far as to say, "On
the contrary, the members of the body that seem to be weaker
are indispensable, and those members of the body that we think
less honorable we clothe with greater honor, and our less respect-
able members are treated with greater respect" (1 Cor 12:22–23,
NRSVue). Likewise, while Jesus was often disheartened by others' lack of faith, he didn't reproach people for expressing honest
doubt, the story of "doubting Thomas" in John 20 being a paradigm case.[2]

What many of our respondents were longing for was the
power of naming their own reality, "finding their voices." In a
strange way, they were like Moses standing before the burning bush. They saw it burning, and wanted to give it a name,
and all they had heard was "I am what I am," "I will be what I
will be," "I will make happen what happens." On the other hand,
they found all the names that they had received from "the tradition" to be limiting, if not pernicious. Still, they wanted to
have *some* way of talking about their deepest experiences, and
the language they had found and used was often that of love in
action. They were comfortable neither with impersonal language
nor with thinking of God as *a* person; if anything, they were
seeking a *trans-* or *supra*-personal idiom that they hadn't found
anywhere.

I really struggle with the word "God," it's kind of baggage
for me, and "higher power" sounds too loosey-goosey.

—*Heidi**

I believe in "something," but I don't know what it is.

*—Anna**

I was very much into Jesus. We talked about my decon-
struction and I think I still believe in God, but it's not
any one version of Him or Her or It. I guess when I think
of God, I think of the love, like the energy of love or
goodness—those kinds of things, not like a person or
something like that.

*—Naomi**

In this, they are standing firmly on one side of Christian tradition, even if they aren't aware of it. The apophatic or negative
perspective acknowledges our inability to know God in, so to
speak, "Godself." It stretches from the Hebrew scriptures through
the era of the medieval mystics—one of the core texts of medieval mysticism is the anonymous fourteenth-century *Cloud of
Unknowing*—and even into the present day, with statements like
that of theologian John Caputo that "God can happen anywhere."[3]
Even the language we traditionally use to describe God, words
like "infinite," "omniscient," and "eternal," says more about what
God (at least to human comprehension) is *not* than about who
or what God is. After all, who among us can really imagine the
infinite?

And in case we think that this is a fringy offshoot of Christianity, we can find a perfectly vivid sense of God's incomprehen-
sibility in St. Augustine, who was surely as much of a taproot for
Western Christianity as anyone since St. Paul. In the opening of
his *Confessions*, Augustine muses:

> Yet how shall I call to my God, the God who is my Lord,
> when it is precisely to me that I am calling him [sic] when
> I call, and what in me is large enough for God to enter?
> How can he who made heaven and earth come into me? Is

there anything in me that can hold you? Can even heaven and earth, which you have made, and in which you hold me, hold you? Or since nothing that is can exist without you, do all things that exist hold you?[4]

This sounds surprisingly like a comment from one of our respondents who said:

> But, believe me, it's been a whole life path of back and forth, and I'm just not in a comfortable place to really know whom I'm even speaking to. And that's where I'm at.
>
> —Dave*

As theologian Catherine Keller puts it:

> To you, God, we say *you*, not knowing quite where the pronoun lands. You lend a perspective on everything else. Or to put this more honestly: you *are* a perspective on everything, except perhaps on yourself. I do not see, hear, smell, or touch you. Except maybe always, everywhere, and therefore indiscernibly... This faith will not morph into the guarantee. The end, from the perspective of the infinite, is endless and thus cannot be secured, predicted, or determined in advance. Each end will fade into its perspectival infinity. We won't take certainty from this cloud of refuge, even when it shines. We might take heart.[5]

For Augustine, and Keller, and many others, this isn't a rhetorical flourish, but rather a deep probe into the limits of human understanding. And when our conversation partners talk about "doing the inner work," Augustine stands right there with them, staring into the abyss, as he often calls his own mind and heart, ready to take the plunge.

It's sobering to note that many of our respondents thought that they could only do this work by turning to Eastern religions or various strategies for self-improvement, never having been told that there were abundant resources within their own tradition of origin.

Many of our respondents thought that they could only do this work by turning to Eastern religions or various strategies for self-improvement, never having been told that there were abundant resources within their own tradition of origin.

I guess I've come to find that the thing I really liked the most about church was that spiritual feeling when you're worshiping or when you're praying... kind of like connecting with something bigger, but I guess I've found other ways of achieving that feeling through meditating or self-reflection or other things to get that same kind of connected spiritual feeling.

—*Tim**

I think I have a lot of things that are very spiritual. I have a community from the friend group that some people might find in a church, and I do a lot of yoga, and I have a lot of questions of like our place in the universe...

—*Taylor**

In a seeming paradox, this indicates that we may open the conversation more authentically, and actually be more faithful, by humbly acknowledging our own *unknowing* than by claiming to know more than we do. How different would the situation often have been if, instead of being told that certain concerns and questions were off limits, the response had been *Say more about that?* Many of our conversation partners frankly acknowledged, and were eager to discuss, the wonder and mystery they found at the core of life, but they had not found people of open minds and hearts with whom they could do so. When we asked them the questions in the survey, they often responded at considerable length, and said something like, "Wow, these are really tough questions. Thanks for asking! There's no other place where I talk about these things."

> **Many of our conversation partners frankly acknowledged, and were eager to discuss, the wonder and mystery they found at the core of life, but they had not found people of open minds and hearts with whom they could do so... "Thanks for asking! There's no other place where I talk about these things."**

When our respondents did have what might be called a residual or vestigial view of God, it was generally that of a stern, punitive, rule-giving father who knew all, saw all, and judged all. Or, as a kind of reaction to and mirror image of that, they held to some version of Moralistic Therapeutic Deism (MTD), as described by Christian Smith, Melinda Lundquist Denton, Richard Flory, and their collaborators in the National Study of Youth and Religion. The original version of MTD included five points:

1. A God exists who created and orders the world and watches over human life on earth.

2. God wants people to be good, nice, and fair to each other, as taught in the Bible and by most world religions.

3. The central goal of life is to be happy and to feel good about oneself.

4. God does not need to be particularly involved in one's life except when God is needed to resolve a problem.

5. Good people go to heaven when they die.[6]

In their most recent formulation of this "cultural spirituality," which they call "Moralistic Therapeutic Deism 2.0," study collaborators have developed seven core tenets:

1. Karma is real

2. Everybody goes to heaven

3. It's all good

4. Religion is easy

5. Just do good

6. Morals are self-evident

7. No regrets[7]

In this view, God, to the extent that God exists at all, is remote and ineffectual, a pale shadow of the God of Abraham, Isaac, and Jacob—essentially "a copy of a copy of a copy," to quote our earlier conversation partner. In other words, "God" is basically a knock-off version of the first person of the Trinity. Perhaps most striking of all, study authors report that while the ways these basic tenets are combined may depend on individual experiences, they "are present among most emerging adults, regardless of where they could be classified, from religiously committed to not religious."[8]

On the other hand, many of our conversation partners expressed great admiration and even affection for Jesus, in the sense that they resonated with him even while they drew a sharp line between him and the church. In an odd way, they might have agreed with theologian Thomas Torrance's suggestion that "There is no dark unknown God behind the back of Jesus Christ."[9] At the same time, they not surprisingly took a "low," ground-level view of Jesus, seeing him as one who had lived an exemplary and inspiring life without necessarily viewing him as God in the flesh. In this, our conversation partners were not all that different from the people Ann Christie and her colleagues interviewed in their study *Ordinary Christology*, "ordinary Christians" who consider themselves faithful and have received no formal training in theology. Christie reports that a majority of her team's survey sample did not consider Jesus to be God. "They do not appear to have learned this doctrine," she explains, "or the related doctrines of pre-existence and the immanent Trinity. They do not conceptualize Jesus's identity in the belief that he was both God and man." Respondents understood the incarnation as "the incarnation of God's creative, revelatory, and salvific power in the person of Jesus Christ; but not a doctrine of the incarnation understood as the incarnation of God the Son, second person of the Trinity." In other words, Christie explains, their Christology was functional rather than ontological.[10]

As *Layla** put it, in a similar vein:

> Jesus was like a very super-awesome man, he was probably super in union with the universe and the world around him and he embodied that energy, but I don't think he was necessarily better than anyone else that way. He just had a natural tendency toward embodying the universe and guidance, etc.

Another, *Aubrey**, asked, somewhat plaintively:

> Do you think there is a place for people like me who are spiritual but not religious but love Jesus?

Again, there are plenty of precedents for this view among those early Christians who referred to themselves simply as followers of "the Way," and whose first confession of faith was "Jesus is Lord." While not all of us may want to limit ourselves to what Christie calls a functional Christology, such a view might open the way to a productive dialogue between practicing members of faith communities and those who consider themselves nones and dones.

B. Possible Common Ground for Further Conversation

From what we have just seen, we suggest some ways in which people of all religious persuasions, and of none at all, could talk productively about "deep questions":

i. Awe/Wonder

Our conversation partners had a deep sense of wonder, and they didn't know where to "put" it. Philosopher Paul Woodruff puts this under the category of "reverence" as a disposition toward awe, accompanied by a sense of human fallibility and finitude, with or without an attachment to a religious tradition. He observes that "Reverence sets a higher value on truth than on any human product that is supposed to have captured the truth."[11] This attitude is more than, for instance, being wowed by a particularly beautiful sunset; it involves a sense that one is somehow *accountable* for one's life and actions. Both members of faith communities and those with no such affiliation might find plenty to discuss around what they regard with reverence in this sense.

ii. Aesthetics/Ritual

A number of people spoke appreciatively of the power of ritual, especially among those who had been raised Catholic,

Episcopalian, and Orthodox, and to some extent, Lutheran. This was the part they missed most about no longer participating in corporate worship.

> I don't know if I ever really believed the dogma and stories and stuff. I always saw it as a lens—maybe I shouldn't say I always saw it, but I always felt this and have only recently found the words to express it. I've always seen it as more of a lens through which our culture is reflected, like the stories that are in the Bible, the collections, the things that Christians talk about. When you really boil them down to the themes, they're the same stories that have been told by every culture throughout the dawn of recorded history. I never thought I was saved thinking about whether the communion wafer actually becomes the body of Christ. I don't think it does, I never thought it did. I thought that stuff was cool, though... I always thought the words, and how dramatic they were, and the lyrics we would sing in the choir were super beautiful and evocative.
>
> —Ed*

In this regard, Woodruff has noted that "Ritual is more robust than belief and has more staying power, but wherever there is ritual, there should be the reverence to take that ritual seriously." Otherwise, he explains "the ritual becomes dry and useless, withers away or becomes a mask for irreverent behavior.[12]

In other words, ritual derives from and depends on a deep sense of awe and reverence, whether or not that reverence has a definite object in mind; simply "going through the motions," which is the way many of our respondents described their experience of church, deserves the bad press it gets.

iii. Spirit

A robust idea of the Holy Spirit might help to bridge the gap between the "spiritual" and the "religious." After all, with its various nuances of wind, breath, life force, etc., and its (his? her?) ambiguous "personhood," the Spirit resists definition—it really does "blow where it will," per John 3:8—and creates a kind of open, dynamic space that resonates with the "something" to which some of our conversation partners refer. In addition, we heard frequent references to the feminine side of God from our respondents, and the recent emphasis by feminist theologians on Spirit in the Bible (the Hebrew *hochma* and the Greek *Sophia*, or "wisdom," and the Hebrew word *ruach*, "wind, spirit" are, after all, feminine) could open some significant doors here.

Is it possible that we are facing, not the eclipse or "end" of Christianity, but rather another form of indigenization, the kind of thing that has happened from time to time since the Jewish church had to wrestle with the possibility that even gentiles were included in the New Covenant? Especially with the rise of Pentecostalism and renewalism in the global church, we may well be looking at a new work of the Spirit among us. What would happen, for example, if we included this Pygmy creed in our regular worship?

> *In the beginning was God.*
> *Today is God.*
> *Tomorrow will be God.*
> *Who can make an image of God?*
> *He* [sic] *has no body.*
> *He is a word that comes out of your mouth.*
> *That word! It is no more.*
> *It is past, and still it lives!*
> *So is God.*[13]

We're not talking about rejecting or repudiating anything. What we are talking about is a renewed emphasis on the Spirit, which has been relatively underemphasized in Western Protestant Christianity. While many of our churches have focused on God the Father and Jesus the Son, the Spirit has often been, as some have said, "the Cinderella of the Trinity," and has been largely sidelined. There is certainly enough room in the Christian world to remedy this situation.

iv. Practices, Virtues, Dispositions, and Attitudes

These were generally viewed as much more important expressions of genuine faith than religious "concepts" of whatever kind. Practices (singing in the choir, going on mission trips, working for social justice, etc.) and being part of a community were generally more important to respondents than particular beliefs, which were often seen as irrelevant or even detrimental to faith. At best, doctrines were valued for their expressive or emotive power. Emerging generations tend to behave, belong, and believe differently and are seeking others with whom to wonder, ask questions, and continue the conversation.

C. Key Points for Reflection for the Church

Previous chapters have included a summary of their content. In this chapter, however, we find that the best "summary" incorporates food for thought regarding how the church might engage what we've learned from our respondents above.

- Provide small group opportunities (preferably around food!). The Dinner Church model is a good template for this. Many of our respondents mentioned how welcome they had found our conversations and said that they felt more comfortable talking about big questions in small groups. Again, the aim in creating such a common ritual would not be something like "fake it till you make it," in the hope that we might eventually segue into something more conventionally "Christian" (as in, "this is *really* the Lord's Supper"), but rather to create an authentic space for the meeting of minds and hearts.[14]

- More broadly, work with people to find creative ways to ritualize and "bless" significant moments in their lives, not only the big ones, but little ones—the death of a pet, the first day of school, passing a driver's test.

- Pay attention to the affective side of faith. This doesn't mean using gimmicks to manipulate people's emotions; it does mean speaking to their hearts as well as their heads. This involves creating spaces in which people can put their "whole self in." Helpful suggestions for doing this can be found in Marcia McFee's *Think Like a Filmmaker*. Some of our respondents said that what they had found most meaningful on those occasions when they attended church was the beauty of the music and the liturgy. As we have noted before, gathering around significant works of art, and creating our own, can be a very effective way to get in touch with and share the affective side of life.

- Further, add "orthopathy" (right feeling) to your list of working definitions, along with orthodoxy (right belief) and orthopraxis (right action). Many of our respondents spoke of the disconnect they found between what church people say and how they actually act; aligning hearts with minds and hands is essential. The emphasis in many of our congregations on Christian *formation* is definitely on the right track here, as is recent literature on family systems in the church and emotionally healthy congregations.

- Get to know some spiritual directors in your area. Spiritual Directors International can help you find a director from a wide range of religious and spiritual traditions—including "spiritual but not religious." Directors are trained in deep, nonjudgmental listening, and can speak to groups of interested persons about what spiritual direction is and isn't. Despite the title, much of a spiritual director's training involves learning how to help people tune into and go with the "God moments" in their lives, without *directing* them.

- Recognize, and emphasize, that faith is not one thing, nor is it a commodity that one simply "has" or doesn't have. There are a lot of different types of spiritualities. For instance, inventories such as the Myers-Briggs Type Indicator (MBTI), the Enneagram, or the DISC inventory, are listed in the bibliography with specific websites for further information on how to link personality type with spiritual disciples. There are stages and seasons of faith, and different styles of prayer and other spiritual disciplines will be appropriate for different people (see 1 Corinthians 12, and check out the Psalms for a real roller coaster of faith). Jesus never said, "Sign the following faith statement." He did say, "Follow me."

D. For Further Group Discussion

1. How have your beliefs changed?

2. Much of the vocabulary used in the worship and life of the church consists of insider talk (grace, sin,

salvation, stewardship, benediction, etc.) that is foreign, if not actually repugnant, to other people.

a. Make a list of such "church words."

b. Can we breathe new life into these words by sharing
a story that explains your experience of them?

c. Can you think of a way to express them in ordinary
language (and, if not, is it possible that you too are a
bit fuzzy on their meaning)?

3. Are there aspects of the list of characteristics of Moralistic Therapeutic Deism (pp. 141–42) that resonate
with you? Is anything missing?

4. Who/what is God/the sacred for you? Has this changed
at various times in your life?

5. Where and how do you experience sacredness?

6. How would you respond to the idea, suggested by
theologian John Caputo, that "God can happen
anywhere"?

7. How does your experience of the sacred express your
ethics of goodness? What does it mean to live a "good"
life?

... YEAH... A CONTINUING CONCLUSION

Sue Pizor Yoder & Brandon M. Heavner, Authors
Joanne P. Marchetto, Editor

"So... this is the question of my life. Rather than one meaning, there are many. Because it is a mystery, a continuous journey, creating meaning, layering on, what is important to us, continuing to ask the question."

—*Elizabeth**

"What does meaning mean? We're making it up as we go. Yeah."

—*Anthony**

A. BELONGING EVERYWHERE, BELONGING NOWHERE

So... what have we learned from our conversations and research? It is alarming and often bewildering to people who have deeply loved their faith communities and dedicated their lives to serve God that nones and dones are the fastest growing "religious" group in America. Faith communities ask, "How can this be?" Yet each successive generation has a growing number of people who do not find the traditional, institutional expressions of religious belief helpful. Concurrently, nones and dones are seeking the very things that faith communities have traditionally offered: ritual, community, and a place where they are loved and belong. *Aurora** shares, "There are communities everywhere, so you can belong to 750,000 different ones, but not really belong to any... so yeah." Or as *Chloe** revealed:

> Our generation struggles with connecting deeply with others. Affected by social media and technology, we're not so much meeting face-to-face. I'm into researching this. We aren't making meaning in the way that relationships give us meaning; we're lacking that right now. And we are lacking the ability to really connect with people. We struggle to make true connections, knowing that everyone has 50, 100, or 700 friends they can talk to at any time. It makes friends seem very disposable at times. It is harder to make meaning in relationships knowing that other people may not feel about you the way you're feeling connected to them... yeah.

Unlike earlier generations,[1] nones and dones from emerging generations want to construct their own beliefs and rituals. As *Thomas** shared: "Our generation is not afraid to say what's on our minds, how we feel. We make our own path, and we don't feel like we have to do as our parents did. The leap of faith in our generation is to let it ride and see what happens... yeah." They are often open to conversations about God, a higher being, a force, and they want the conversations to be truly "open" without judgment, dogma, or tenets declaring a predetermined outcome. They experience themselves to be thoughtful, caring, and compassionate and are deeply troubled when people assume the opposite because they either do not believe in God or have yet to determine *what it is that they believe.*

So, what *are* they looking for? What have we learned? For one thing, they are looking for communities that create a safe place to explore, question, doubt, and wonder about what they believe instead of heading for safety, certainty, or pat answers. They have found it rare to locate a faith community that entertains possibilities and wonderments instead of stopping at doctrine and creed. Emerging generations are stifled when faith communities do not engage their own beliefs and convictions as expansive playgrounds for growth, discovery, and possibility. *Elizabeth** shared, "This is the question of my life... rather than one meaning, there are many. Because it is a mystery, a continuous journey, creating meaning, layering on, what is

> **We discovered that many of our conversation partners have not left religion behind; rather, they are finding religion outside of its institutions.**

important to us, continuing to ask the questions." Communities that avoid labels, avoid putting people in boxes or making them feel like they are someone's project, are attractive. Nones and dones want the focus of a faith community to be on what its people *embody* instead of what they oppose. They value the interconnectedness of the world, nature, and humanity. They appreciate when room is allowed for things sensed but not proven, intuited but not defined, and they are quite comfortable with ambiguity and not knowing. Communities that integrate learnings from science, psychology, philosophy, and insights of world religions appeal to nones and dones. We discovered that many of our conversation partners have not left religion behind; rather, they are finding religion outside of its institutions. We heard these important statements:

- Our conversation partners are incredibly open to role models and mentors with embodied beliefs who will engage them honestly, treat them as equals, and help them to name and pursue their passions.

- They value and desire experiential expressions of faith that involve their senses, creativity, the arts, and the engagement of their hearts—not just their heads.

- They are open to or looking for brave spaces where they can talk about the things that are relevant and important to their lives.

- They long for communities where they can be their authentic selves and feel accepted and loved. Their values include egalitarian communities where women, minorities, LGBTQIA+, and those who are differently abled are all truly welcomed, and where all have equal voice and power in decision-making.

- The *integration* of their world, nature, and humanity is a critical core value.

- They want their lives to matter and to pursue causes worth fighting for.

- They are looking for communities that own their past mistakes and have a plan to change for the future.

Nones and dones' perceptions of the church often catch faith communities unaware! We heard reflected over and again these thoughts and experiences:

- Denominations and church hierarchies are authoritarian and outdated.

- Religious institutions function as dispensers of knowledge rather than communities of discovery.

- Churches are homophobic. Nones and dones appreciate the message that God wants us to "love our neighbor," and yet they experience that church people reject and condemn that very same neighbor.

- Faith communities are too politically partisan. Nones and dones strongly feel that political parties and faith expressions should NOT be indecipherable from one another.

- Churches are intolerant of diversity and hold restrictive doctrines and dogmatic stances. Nones and dones would like to experience openness to discovery and mystery (a place to name one's doubts, questions, and fears).

- Those brought up in faith communities found the foundational stories of faith were not presented to them in helpful, applicable, or relevant ways. When they asked questions, most were shut down.

- Sadly, the most frequent words we heard used to describe their experiences within faith communities were irrelevant, judgmental, rigid, boring, stuck, homophobic, intolerant, and sexist.

We realized through our conversations with our interviewees that we hold much in common regarding our values, and we are all asking remarkably similar questions. What we are not doing is asking those related questions together in shared dialogical community. While we learned this first from three years of reading, researching, and reflecting, we *really* learned this by listening to our interviewees' stories.

B. LIVING THE STORY

Do not underestimate the power of story. Stories can be long, short, serious, funny, ancient, contemporary, dark, inspirational, even captivating! Each person and community has their own unique story to tell—countless journeys, quests, memories, and experiences all waiting to be told and retold. In the words of author Sue Monk Kidd, "Stories have to be told or they die, and when they die, we can't remember who we are or why we're here."[2] People of faith have told their traditional and ancestors' stories for generations because they believe they have heard and experienced something transformative in them that is important to pass on. Ancient faith stories from different traditions record people's journey in this physical realm and with those that inhabit the spiritual realm and the tangled relationship between the two. If told well, and discussed openly and honestly, the wisdom of these stories can speak to the experience of our lives. For our conversation partners, no single or permanent body of stories received fixed or authoritative prominence. They prefer interpreting, remixing, and even adapting these stories.

Mark Wingfield discusses how emerging generations are "unbundling" their faith.[3] An "unbundled faith" does not rely on a single tradition or organization to inform a person's religious beliefs and practices. Rather, it is a mosaic of various traditions, not necessarily religious, expressive of a single person's convictions as opposed to a communal dogma or doctrine.[4] Biblical stories are engaged as *stories*, held on an equal footing with others: myths, fables, poetry, autobiographies, video games, '90s gangsta rap, Broadway musicals—even a favorite comic book cinematic universe. So, what we have done is to rediscover the power of *all* stories, and invited you to listen in on what we have learned from our conversation partners along with our research.

C. CHAPTERS REVISITED

We asked about the stories that shaped the lives of our conversation partners to learn what inspires them and shapes their worldview. Life is a journey. For the people represented in this book, the majority identified family, or an event connected with family, as significant influences in their current identity. It was a privilege to hear their stories and to see what they value, how they make sense of the world, and how they refer to themselves. We found this distinguishing characteristic for the generations that our conversation partners represent; they are comfortable blurring the lines demarcating sexual orientation, gender identity, religious beliefs, political parties, and ethnicity. Our world is becoming more densely interconnected as people travel widely, and innovative technology alongside the rise of social media have closed the geographic distance between people. Each day brings new exposure to different value systems, cultural mores, belief systems, and diverse languages spoken around us. These shifts are changing how younger generations understand who they are and how they relate to others.

Navigating these shifts creates and cultivates places—physical and communal—where we experience the story of belonging. We all have a basic human need to belong. Historically people in the United States found belonging through faith communities and ethnic affiliation. As second and third generations scattered and acclimated to America, families grew more diverse. We became a nation of "joiners" in civic organizations, political involvement, and faith membership within our neighborhoods. However, compounding societal changes continue to influence every facet of our lives, resulting in a reshuffling of our social capital and networks. People long for a place where they experience acceptance, love, and inclusion in the midst of diversity. Community organizations can strive to offer a safe space for people to explore and become their best selves. Emerging generations are open to humble mentoring relationships that could facilitate this desired love and acceptance.

The inherited values that resonate prominently among emerging generations are expressed through the various forms of media that inspire, captivate, and engage these shared human desires. Our conversation partners and our research showed us that emerging generations want to be content cocreators. They did not regard any single or permanent body of stories (in whatever medium) as fixed or sacred, and all stories remain open to interpretation, remixing, and even parody. To have fruitful dialogue, people of faith need to understand that, for nones and dones, sacred stories exist on an equal footing with others' stories. People of traditional faith need to trust the sacred story without controlling a specific outcome.

In the sharing of stories, we discover that adversity comes to all of us. People from emerging generations are facing adversity through support systems of family and friend networks, and we discovered they are more open and honest about how their struggles affect them mentally, socially, and emotionally than were previous generations. Vulnerability can foster empathy. Family systems thinking, described in chapter 4, teaches us to hold the complexity of life's challenges, develop resiliency, promote healing, and continue in life. Stories of personal adversity as well as stories from our sacred traditions can build understanding of life's complexities. Our conversation partners' favorite stories were diverse, interactive, and reflected their values and experiences. These are stories in their most accessible sense, through which they establish and maintain their identity and values and create a sense of listening and community.

A story of legacy remains incomplete. Our conversation partners shared their hopes to be remembered as good people, defining "goodness" to include kindness, generosity, and helpfulness to those around them. They express "the good" through empathic listening and cultivating ritual spaces for others to encounter and experience wonder in community. These values help to create the foundation for authentically sharing our personal and collective stories. Such a legacy does not stem from a desire for celebrity, but a hope of leaving the world—or at least our small part of it—a better place. Our conversation partners called on faith communities to *live* the tenets of our faith. This is the challenge to faith communities: to pass on the traditional stories instead of continuing to develop institutions as the primary means for leaving a legacy to future generations.

When it comes to the beliefs and practices that accompanied our conversation partners through various stages of their life stories, one of the biggest differences articulated was not between the religiously unaffiliated and church folk. In fact, growing numbers of people in the church do agree with nones and dones and find the traditional formulations of faith incomprehensible, if not offensive. Our respondents were often quite willing to discuss their spiritual experiences with us; at the same time, they did not have, or want to use, preconceived language or concepts in doing so. In this, they sounded surprisingly like those figures in Jewish, Christian, and other traditions who have talked about their *experiences* of God without feeling a need to *describe* God. Our conversation partners encounter "God" in actions and relationships rather than in beliefs or concepts.

D. THE CONVERSATION CONTINUES...

Across generations and faith traditions, there is a yearning to experience inspiration from communities where roots can grow deep and values are passed on in an enduring, endearing way. This process of living in shared story becomes its own ritual, which makes living the story even more interesting and sharing the story even more necessary.

As we engaged in this process, Co.lab.inq appreciated the value of listening to our interviewees tell their stories. We could relate at various times to our partners' stories of judgment and pain. Some of us grew up in atmospheres of openness, wonderment, inquisitiveness, and ever-expanding ideas about God. Others reflected on experiences of being shut down, told to quit asking so many questions, or being confronted by an authoritarian figure who closed off all awe and mystery. We came to appreciate our conversation partners' desire for community: a safe place to explore what they believe and where they could ask their tough questions, raise doubts, and know they will not be ostracized when they risk doing so. Their stories often made us uncomfortable, and yet there was great power in sharing them in a nondefensive, judgment-free zone that facilitated understanding and connection.

Stories are fluid and expansive, flexible and human. They invite us to adapt, to imagine the storyteller's environment and experience. Upon listening to, reading, and rereading our conversation partners' stories, we realized that there are no easy solutions or answers to the issues they are raising. In fact, that may not be the point. They are not right or wrong; they just are. We may need to create a whole new language. For instance, many of those whom we have referred to as nones and dones are perhaps more accurately described as "umms," as pastor and seminary professor Mike Moore recently discussed in *Christianity Today*.[5] Moore refers to a growing body of people who want to return to a local faith body, but feel stuck, demotivated, and discouraged by the current state of their local faith communities. Post-pandemic, their engagement with faith communities hasn't moved into the realm of decisive demarcation like nones or dones, but remains an expression of hesitancy, because the values and practices expressed in faith communities around them have left them going, "umm....." As one young woman states in Brian McLaren's recent book *Faith After Doubt*:

> [Faith communities] want the "millennials" like me to come and save them. But really, they want us less as members or partners and more as fuel to keep their operation going. So, people like me give up on church entirely and join the "nones," which means that the demand stays low

for faith communities that welcome people with questions and doubts and want to focus on love instead. It's a self-perpetuating downward spiral.... I want to be part of a community that isn't obsessed with saving their own damned souls, but that actually wants to try to save this world that we're on the verge of destroying. So...[6]

Our team hears incredible *hope* in this young woman's cry. Also consider the invitation to hope found in *Brynn's** interview:

For people in general, religion was good. It gave people something to believe in and steered people in the right direction to do good in the world. What has happened to me has happened to a lot in my generation. Because we're not as bound to our religion, the consequences are not going to the community each week, seeing some people. Because we do not participate in church, maybe we don't participate in the community so much, or do kind acts. Maybe that's why we're so broken. If more faiths were open—not as judgmental—more people would participate and join.

Listening further to *Jose's** story, he continues his search for meaning:

I want to make clear that, despite being an atheist and having this opinion about faith, God, higher being, it is a void in me. Some people fill the void with organized religion, and it helps them find meaning, but I've tried and still it wasn't there for me. The interesting question is, what is the point of this if there's no before and after? Spirituality and religion force you to find more of a reason to get up and get going each day.

E. IDEAS FOR CONSIDERATION

We have tried to stay away from being too prescriptive in our suggestions. People make connections and enter spaces of shared vulnerability differently. However, there are appropriately consistent guiding principles that will help us all assume the task of embodying our shared story. These principles will be both challenging and enlivening for everyone: nones, dones, "umms," and faith communities. We learned from our interviewees that they want to be content cocreators. Before

There is no detailed set of instructions for how to make this work: It is an adaptable process with no technical solutions.

the conversation begins, invite them into the process. There is no detailed set of instructions for how to make this work: It is an adaptable process with no technical solutions.

Managerial consultant Ronald A. Heifetz famously claims that leading institutional change is a process of "disappointing people at a rate they can absorb."[7] Dredging up memories of pain, abuse, and trauma will be disappointing. Hearing perspectives that challenge, critique, or criticize will be frustrating. Encountering people who do not agree with your worldview, share your deepest held convictions, or understand the nuances of your personal lived experiences will be upsetting. To be the change we want to see in the world, we will need to risk wading into the deep end of the pool. This intentional relationship-building will push, poke, prod, stretch, and disappoint people if we do it well.

Wading into a body of water takes time—one step at a time, to be exact. It's the rate we can absorb. The tendency may be to want to dive in head-first, but that is never advisable in unfamiliar waters. The "deep waters" may be shallower than you think, and you never know what kind of undercurrent could sweep you away toward undesirable peril, convincing you to scramble back out, swearing off swimming ever again.

Wade! When the water is just a bit too cold for comfort, the initial shock catches us suddenly, forcing our bodies to recoil and adjust. There will be moments when we need to stop and linger at one spot or another to better acclimate to the temperature and the current, but only long enough to adequately prepare for the next step. *Sempre avanti*, always forward, because we cannot go backward; we must go forward to participate in the story. Otherwise, the story will not be told, and those who come after will be no closer to solving the mystery than we are today. Thank goodness we are all going to be disappointed together. It gives us the opportunity to strive for something at a rate we can all absorb.

As you carve out space to cultivate these rich, meaningful, transformative relationships through intentional conversations, here are eight things Co.lab.inq encountered for ourselves as our conversation partners invited us to go beyond our comfort zone. We offer them to you as collective insight and wisdom, hoping that as you begin the journey with others, you do not succumb to discouragement the first time you meet disappointing resistance.

- The challenge for the church is to listen and embrace each other and our stories and find points of connection. Religiously affiliated and unaffiliated persons need to look outside their primary sources of inspiration to discover and embrace the best humanity has to offer, developing points of connection as we rally around shared luminaries who exemplify the best of our common existence.

- Ideally, faith communities know that all people long for a place to be their authentic, whole selves, and should strive to offer safe places for people to explore and become their best selves. Emerging generations are open to humble mentoring relationships that could facilitate this desired love and acceptance.

- Sharing and hearing stories of adversity from the past and from our sacred traditions can help us understand each other, creating a sense of listening and community that meets and develops resiliency in the face of adversity.

- Those of us within faith communities can choose to focus on living the tenets and keeping the stories of our faith alive rather than maintaining established institutions for organizational survival.

- If you are part of a faith community in decline, consider laying everything on the table for discussion and possibility. Invite people from your community to engage in active conversation with you about how you might begin to serve the needs of your community. If you are a none, done, or umm, consider taking the risk to approach a local faith community with a conversation about how you might potentially partner together for the well-being of your neighborhood.

- In chapter 3, we discussed the impact of living in what Zygmunt Bauman called "liquid" culture, in which all is in flux and there are no fixed boundaries. Talk to others with whom you have not yet developed relationships and listen to their stories.

- Share your stories about what is important to you in your faith community. Explore opportunities to meet with your neighbors and share the stories of what is important to each of you.

- Our team could author additional books based on the amount of research we have gathered. What else do you suggest needs to be researched? Write to us at co.lab.inq@gmail.com and share your thoughts.

We are a group of faith leaders who are trying to be honest about what we have seen, heard, and learned. We want to explore what is and is not working within institutional faith communities, for all their good intentions, and open it up for conversation and dialogue. We feel called to share what we have learned, and to confront those parts of institutional religion that allow belief systems and bureaucracies to trump how we care for one another. *Rigidity* in dogma and institutional structures will be the death of our beloved faith communities if permitted to reign supreme. Collaboration, inclusion, acknowledging our interdependence, and sharing our sacred stories instead of declaring their inerrancy must become part of the way we live together. We want to speak openly and compassionately to our siblings in faith because we understand the challenges and changes we are facing in faith communities. Working through the adversity we face in faith communities, we want to listen to everyone's stories. Reflecting on the legacy we want to leave behind, we must also speak prophetically. It is imperative that we transition to the time in which we live. This requires that we listen well to people who are different from us, rather than spending our time and energy in religious ventures that can become exclusive and empty rituals, missing the point of religious practice and community.

Something new is pregnant with possibility; we are hoping a new way of living faith can be born. We are hoping to be midwives. The story of the midwives Shiphrah and Puah (Exodus 1:15–22) gives us an example of courage in the face of fear, caring for individuals with healing and compassion. They walk with us while encouraging us to feel and push through our pain, welcoming calm and focus, and birthing something new.

F.... YEAH...

Another interjectory word commonly used in our interviews which is the bane of any English teacher's existence: the non-standard spelling of yes, most fondly spoken as "yeah." "Yeah" appeared in our conversation transcripts as both an affirmation of all things spoken in truth, honesty, and vulnerability, as well as a capstone sentiment that hung in the air after a particularly poignant response to our seven inquiries. "Yeah" functioned to allow those sharing to reflect on the impact of their responses in their own lived experiences, from trauma, pain, and heartache, to joy, relief, and gratitude. "Yeah" bookended many responses, where they held the beginning and end of a thought in tension between two colloquially shared interjectors. And more than one concluded their responses (some to every one of our inquiries) with the reflection, "so... yeah... ," leaving their thoughts to trail off into the ether of the safe, sacred space we had shared with one another.

"Yeah" underscores so much about both the process we, Co.lab.inq, fostered as we engaged volumes of written material and hours of deep, intentional conversations with one another and with our conversation partners. Like a personal story, "yeah" refuses to be denied, dismissed, or devalued because it is affirmation in its purest form. This happened. This is real. This is my experience. In sharing stories and engaging in conversation, we cannot know the nuances of any person's lived experience as fully as they do, because it is theirs alone. We can only glimpse a piece of what gets shared freely and vulnerably, and in that space, offer mutual consolation and affirmation that this, too, is a part of this world in which we live. Hearing, reflecting, and celebrating the wisdom and insights shared by our interviewees, we found that more often than not, the affirmative "yeah" was echoed among us in response to the truth shared with us by a group that, self-identifying as religiously none or done, has in many ways become an object of study rather than people of intrinsic value and intrigue.

So...

Yeah, your stories of inspiration inspire us to connect with more people so that we can nurture one another with positive, world-changing dynamism and passion.

Yeah, your expressions of belonging and meaningful relationships make us want to participate in and contribute to a place that is just as meaningful and just as powerful for us and for those closest to us.

Yeah, your favorite piece of media shares a great story about the timeless values and virtues we hope all people can identify with and embody, so much so that we want to immerse ourselves in the reality of that poem, film, novel, game, or song so that we can better understand how you see the world and share in that bliss alongside you.

Yeah, the obstacles you have endured, and the adversities thrown your way, make us want to scream and cry and flip over tables and set the world on fire. We know those feelings of betrayal and heartbreak too, and we don't want anyone to experience such a hellish event ever again.

Yeah, we too have thought about what we want to leave behind when we die, and hope and pray that our legacy is something worthy of celebration as a benefit for all who may come after us.

Yeah, we are people of faith who have done our fair share of lamenting the atrocities committed in, among, and by faith communities, and have experienced our own portion of disappointment from being given prescribed answers, but somehow, we sometimes can't seem to do the basic "love one another" thing that Jesus guy talked so much about.

Yeah, we hear you. Yeah, we see you. We know where some of the hurt is, and you are not alone. We are all trying to do better; to be better.

"So" is the great invitation, "yeah," the great bridge. By this point in the book, we hope you have accepted the invitation and listened in on a small fraction of the conversations.

We invite you to be the "so" and welcome others into this process of discovery, curiosity, inquiry, and collaboration. Be the bridge that keeps the conversation moving, and not stuck at a gap on the path. We have offered a set of tools that worked well for us to help facilitate this meaningfully generative process of mystery, wonder, and learning. Carry them on into your own communities, with your own neighbors, and see the riches awaiting discovery as you share life with one another. Thanks for hearing us out.

So... yeah...

APPENDIX 1

ABOUT THE RESEARCH

A. DEFINITIONS

Meaning-making: For this group, meaning-making refers to the struggle or work to understand the existential questions of "Who am I/are we?" and "What is my purpose?" In other words, it is the process of making sense of the world around us and, in particular, the life and situations we find ourselves facing.

This definition contrasts with meaning-making as part of *education and literacy*, which is the process of encoding and decoding materials, data, and discourse for information and knowledge. Included in this are the critical thinking skills required to make sense of learning. Meaning-making as a term is also used in *linguistics, cultural anthropology, and translation studies*, which is the process of understanding semiotics (the theory of signs) and how it relates to the cultural values and systems of behavior and organization to comprehend the information and gain wisdom. Finally, meaning-making in the *counseling and trauma healing field* is the process of reflecting and reshaping our stories to assimilate suffering and pain and discover purposeful direction for one's life.

Nones and Dones: "Nones" refers to those who identify as having no particular religious affiliation or belief system. "Dones" refers to those who have previous experience in a religious community who no longer wish to identify with that religious organization.

Generations: One of the parameters for selecting the interview participants was by generation. This tool allowed us to examine a group of people who have been influenced by a unique set of circumstances and global and regional events, moral and social values, changes in technology and education, and cultural norms and behaviors. "A generation is an analytical tool for understanding culture and the people within it. It simply reflects the idea that people who are born during a certain period of time are influenced by a unique set of circumstances and global event, moral and social values, technologies, and cultural norms and behaviors."[1]

Gen Zers were born between 1996 and 2015.
Millennials were born between 1981 and 1995.
Gen Xers were born between 1965 and 1980.
Boomers were born between 1946 and 1964.
Builders were born prior to 1946.

We interviewed people between the ages of 18 and 40—the Gen Z and millennial generations. A few were younger Gen X members. We initially limited our pool of interviewees to people who had some connection with Eastern Pennsylvania; however, we had some people volunteer to be part of the study who came from our social networks and may not have lived in or around Eastern Pennsylvania.

B. METHODOLOGY
i. Library Research

We read widely to discover what others in the fields of religion, theology, philosophy, entertainment, business and economy, technology and innovation, social science and leadership, and organization were discovering. We did not limit ourselves to books but also read online articles and blog posts. We listened to podcasts and interviewed other religious leaders and researchers on the topics of meaning-making and community formation.

We gathered regularly to discuss our notes and to share our findings. We took time to find similarities and disparities. And we reflected as a group on our personal and professional experiences and the realities we face in our roles and lives, questioning how the library research compared to our experiences.

ii. Research Question

Given the rapid or noted decline in church membership, our group began by asking the question of how nones and dones "make meaning." Through our academic research and conversations, we recognized that we were asking the wrong question. The question of "meaning-making" was far less important to our conversation partners than notions of agency, belonging, authenticity, and values.

iii. Ethnographic Interviews

Ethnography is a qualitative research method designed to study groups of people. It is an immersive form of study where the researcher is within the culture itself. We as researchers are members of Christian communities. Many of Co.lab.inq's members work extensively with persons who are members of different faith traditions as well as others who do not identify with any faith tradition or religious expression. Our goal was to interview people outside the religious community to do a narrative comparative analysis of our common cultural values and our differences. Our goal was to learn from our conversation partners while also raising our self-awareness of our gaps in knowledge, experience, and values.

This research method required us to be honest that we are religious people. We are church people who to one degree or another wish to see the faith of that institution passed on to the next generation. We do not agree on what the church of the future should look like, its structures, its leadership, its theology, or its practices. We all have faith and would like to see it shared with others. Our goal was to identify our commonalities and differences so that we might enter a conversation with our partners to continue the work of shaping the future church.

As our team developed our interview questions, we wanted to learn our conversation partners' values and their ways of making meaning. The questions were open ended. Our intent was to ask questions that could allow our conversation partners to share as openly and honestly as possible without implying any religious bias, and to allow our conversation partners freedom in their responses. Stories are powerful indicators of cultural values. The stories we tell, and how we tell them, give information about values. Stories also communicate our customs as they describe our behaviors and patterns of meaning-making. As the team interviewed our conversation partners, we prepared for uniformity in our presentation of the questions in order to analyze the stories we received. We developed protocols for the interview process and shared them with our partners. We asked permission to record our conversations and use their responses for potential future publication. Most of our partners expressed excitement to hear from us what we learned through this process and asked to be informed if we did write a book.

We also developed a demographic survey. We asked our conversation partners to fill out the survey prior to the questions. This survey asked participants to identify their age, where they live, level of education, gender identity, ethnicity, if they were born in the United States, and faith affiliation (if any).

Our original plan was to conduct these interviews in person and in small group settings. Due to the Covid-19 pandemic, we chose to move to an online format using the Zoom video application. This allowed us to record, transcribe, review, and compile data to find trends. On Zoom, we met with people in both small groups and individually. In some small groups, people did not know each other; in other groups, they did. On average, interviews lasted approximately 15 to 20 minutes per person. After we conducted approximately 10 interviews, our conversation partners asked why we were not asking them about their faith practices. They suggested we add an additional question to our interviews, which we did. We added the sixth question, "If you are a person who has practiced a particular faith tradition, how has your practice changed over the years, if at all?"

After all the interviews were completed with our conversation partners, each member of the team read the transcripts and made notes, looking for quotes, trends, and insights. We evaluated the stories as a team, looking for connections in the stories: connections with our research, with our own experience, and with the experiences of other conversation partners. As we analyzed and reflected on the data, we also engaged in self-awareness practices to be sure we were not looking for trends to confirm our own assumptions. We named our assumptions as we evaluated the stories to allow each partner's story to stand on its own, highlighting the values, customs, and meaning.

Our team also consulted with Marjorie Royle, PhD, a research analyst with The Center for Analytics, Research & Development, and Data (CARDD). She assisted us in compiling the data for review, identifying trends, and providing qualitative analysis.

iv. Experiential Learning Cycles

The book's construction is meant to be an invitation to dialogue as we all work to discover what the future might look like regarding community formation and making meaning. To this end, we chose to follow a discovery process described in David Kolb's experiential learning cycle:[2]

- Shared concrete experience (in the form of stories)

- Reflective observations (identifying themes or areas of confusion or question)

- Abstract conceptualizations (applying theoretical models or added information)

- Active experimentation (offering innovations and alternative practices)

The stories were selected from both the conversation partners' responses to the question and from our own personal experiences. We allowed the stories to intersect or bump up against each other as a means for identifying the commonalities and the divergences, and also to invite the reader to enter into the experience and to reflect on his or her own unique experiences. We offer some impressions and some ideas for innovation and adaptation. We hope to inspire further conversation, exploration, and innovation.

APPENDIX 2

DEMOGRAPHIC DATA

We have included demographic data. This data comes from both the demographic survey and content of the interviews. This is self-reported data from the participants. Some data comes from the demographic survey, and this was combined with information gleaned from the interviews. The participants were not required to answer all the questions, and on rare occasions, some people chose not to answer portions of the questions.

A. OUR INTERVIEW RESPONDENTS (ROLLING SAMPLE) DISTRIBUTION BY AGE

This is the breakdown of the ages of our conversation partners/ interviewees. In the demographic information below, these are the age categories for the quantitative data categories from our demographic survey:

10%	Born before 1980 (older)
72%	Born from 1980 to 1995 (millennial)
18%	Born after 1995 (Gen Z)

i. Education

A majority of our respondents had a college-level education. According to the US Census Bureau data for Lehigh County,

Pennsylvania, 89.5 percent of people aged 25 and older have a high school diploma or higher degree, and 30.8 percent have a college degree or higher level of education.[1] In Northampton County, Pennsylvania, 91.3 percent of people aged 25 and older have a high school diploma or higher degree, and 31.8 percent have a college degree or higher level of education.[2]

This chart reflects the education of participants in our study and matches the census data for both Lehigh and Northampton Counties.

Education	Percentage of Those Responding			
	Total	Older	Millennial	Gen Z
High school diploma	11%	0%	8%	30%
Specialized/Trade Certificate	1%	4%	1%	0%
Associate Degree	7%	18%	6%	8%
Bachelor's Degree	51%	32%	52%	58%
Master's Degree	24%	32%	28%	5%
Doctorate	6%	14%	7%	1%

ii. Sexual Orientation and Gender Identity

The following information relates to the sexual orientation and gender identity our conversation partners reported. Not surprisingly, we discovered that conversation partners in the younger generations hold the categories loosely and are more fluid in selecting gender identity and sexual orientation. In the demographic survey, we chose not to ask a person's sexual orientation, but did ask for the participants' gender identity. Some conversation partners chose to reveal their sexual orientation during the interviews, and this information is included in the Sexual Orientation Table. The "unknown" are those who did not identify themselves during the interview. The Gender Identity Table is based on information provided from the demographic survey.

Sexual Orientation	Percentage of Those Responding			
	Total	Older	Millennial	Gen Z
Straight	34%	36%	33%	38%
LGBT	14%	13%	13%	20%
Unknown	51%	50%	54%	42%

Gender Identity	Percentage of Those Responding			
	Total	Older	Millennial	Gen Z
Female	65%	82%	62%	65%
Male	31%	18%	34%	25%
Binary/Fluid/Other	4%	0%	3%	10%

iii. Immigration Status

In Lehigh County, 11.9 percent of residents are foreign born; that number of people in Northampton County is 7.8 percent.

Immigrant Status	Percentage of Those Responding			
	Total	Older	Millennial	Gen Z
Born outside US	4%	9%	3%	5%
Parent born outside US	9%	9%	8%	12%
At least 2nd generation US	85%	82%	87%	80%
Not in US	2%	0%	2%	2%

iv. Race and Ethnicity

In the Lehigh Valley today, 70 percent of residents identify as white, 21 percent identify as Hispanic or LatinX, 7 percent Black, and 3.5 percent Asian.[3]

Race/Ethnicity	Percentage of Those Responding			
	Total	Older	Millennial	Gen Z
White	78%	86%	77%	75%
White w/ specific ethnicity	9%	9%	9%	5%
African American/Black	3%	0%	4%	2%
African/Caribbean	2.00%	4%	1%	2%
Hispanic/Latinx/Puerto Rican	5%	0%	6%	5%
Asian	2%	0%	1%	5%
Biracial	2%	0%	1%	5%

B. ANALYZING THE DATA

Faith Tradition Growing Up	Percentage of Those Responding			
	Total	Older	Millennial	Gen Z
None	7%	4%	7%	8%
Roman Catholic	22%	27%	21%	20%
Lutheran	14%	14%	14%	10%
Other Mainline Protestant	30%	36%	30%	28%
Evangelical	5%	4%	6%	2%
Protestant/Non-denominational	2%	4%	5%	2%
Christian	6%	4%	6%	10%
Eastern Orthodox	1%	0%	1%	2%
Jewish	1%	0%	1%	0%
Two or more faith traditions	11%	4%	11%	15%

Current faith tradition	Percentage of Those Responding			
	Total	Older	Millennial	Gen Z
Yes	56%	73%	54%	52%
No	18%	4%	19%	20%
Not anymore	16%	14%	14%	25%
Never	2%	0%	3%	0%
Thinking about it	17%	14%	18%	15%

Activity Level	Percentage of Those Responding			
	Total	Older	Millennial	Gen Z
Very active	10%	4%	8%	20%
Loosely active	8%	9%	8%	5%
Attend somewhat	12%	23%	11%	10%
Maybe searching	18%	4%	21%	10%
Mild belief, not active	7%	4%	6%	10%
Spiritual/own religion	19%	36%	19%	10%
Agnostic	10%	4%	7%	22%
Atheist	18%	14%	19%	12%

Current Faith Tradition	Percentage of Those Responding			
	Total	Older	Millennial	Gen Z
Christian	50%	46%	52%	45%
Jewish	1%	4%	1%	0%
Muslim	0%	0%	0%	0%
Buddhist	3%	4%	4%	0%
Hindu	0%	0%	0%	0%
Humanist	11%	32%	11%	0%
None	28%	14%	31%	22%
Agnostic	6%	4%	3%	18%
Spiritual	3%	0%		
Not sure/searching	3%	0%		
Atheist	2%	0%	3%	0%
Pagan/Nature	3%	4%	2%	2%
Unitarian/Universalist	2%	4%	2%	0%
Open-minded/	1%	0%	1%	0%
Have own mix of beliefs	5%	14%	2%	10%
Other	4%	0%	4%	5.00%

For each question, frequency tables were constructed of all themes that were mentioned by more than one interviewee, and cross-tabulations were made to compare responses from Gen Z, millennials, and a comparison group of older adults. Finally, the

KHCoder3 text analysis program was used to produce word frequencies for responses to each question, and key-word-in-context lists were prepared for the most common theme words.

At first glance, the data from our demographic survey may seem to indicate that we did not interview many people who are not affiliated with organized religion (see the charts below). However, the stories that they shared with us indicated that the majority of the conversation partners had either left a faith-based organization or have never been a part of such an organization, and yet many were comfortable talking about God, the divine, and the spiritual realm. This leaves us wondering what the discrepancy indicates.

Here are some of the questions that would need to be explored to dig deeper into the mismatch responses.

- On the one hand, 56 percent of respondents indicated they had a faith tradition, but as their stories revealed, this no longer implies that they participate in a religious institution. Have they already dismissed the institutions from their definition of faith tradition when ticking these boxes?

- Are there cultural implications for the way one asks? Do questions about current faith traditions consciously or subconsciously influence the way people respond when filling in questionnaires? With the resurgence of anti-Semitism and other biases, are we conditioned to check the "acceptable" label to avoid discriminatory practices? Is it easier to check the expected than to make the statement of being a nonconformist? Are they perhaps reluctant to answer, or simply indifferent to this categorization of the population?

- Did we assume, when we set up the list of options, that people understand and have thought through categories such as humanist, spiritual, agnostic, atheist, pagan/nature and could differentiate between them? Filling in this form was their introduction to us and our interview; did they rush through the process so as not to delay the interview? Would they have filled it in differently if we had asked them to do so *after* the interview and *after* they better understood our intentions?

- Most interesting, are these the wrong categories and quite possibly the wrong questions? Would they have given their faith practice a different label—such as mysticism or meditation (being in the moment)? Would they have preferred to answer the question of which practices are they currently or interested in exploring, which allows for fluidity or the openness to faith without boundaries defined by institutions?

It makes sense to use questionnaires or survey forms to help identify our conversation partners in terms of their backgrounds so that we are honest in presenting the portion of society that we interviewed. However, the responses lead us to suspect that the standard categories are outdated, as is obvious when talking about binary sexual orientation or ethnicity in an increasingly multi-ethnic society.

In the words of political scientist Ryan Burge, who analyzes quantitative data to explore the rise of the nones: "One of the things I constantly have to remind myself when I do data analysis is that every single row on my spreadsheet represents a human being who has a story to tell... Whatever their motives, we should be seeking out people willing to tell their stories, inviting them to tell us, and listening—really listening—to them."[4]

ABOUT THE AUTHORS

Sue: I recruited each of these amazing human beings to join me in my journey to understand and make sense of the many changes occurring in the church and the world around it. These colleagues have become dear friends. We've so enjoyed our time with one another that we can't wait to hear your feedback, to write our next book together, and to keep the conversation going. They are too humble to tell you some things about themselves that I thought important for you to know about each of them, so I have added a few comments to give you "the rest of the story."

Rev. Dr. Bonnie Bates
Bonnie: I was raised as a Roman Catholic and moved into the United Church of Christ in 1984. The congregational polity suits me much better. I completed degrees in organization management, human resource development, Master of Divinity, and Doctor of Ministry. I have a passion for church—traditional, creative, virtual, or in-person. As the conference minister for the Penn Northeast Conference of the UCC, I work regularly with congregations seeking to reach out to younger community members. My family's participation in church varies by generation, younger generations not being inclined toward institutional church. Exploration of millennial and Gen X stories is important to my understanding of the lack of participation of these and other age groups.

Sue: Bonnie is open and approachable, honest and dedicated. She loves deeply and often gave us words or images for things we struggled to name. Bonnie lost her dear husband during our time together, which reminded us all of the many losses we are all feeling. She also acquired a precious little puppy that has made us all giggle with delight. The UCC's are lucky to have such a passionate voice dedicated to the voices of those often perceived as the least and last in our culture. She joined our team from many places via Zoom, phone, car, airport, and in person!

Rev. Brandon M. Heavner

Brandon: Born in western North Carolina, I earned a bachelor of arts in religious studies from Lenoir-Rhyne University (LRU) and Master of Divinity from Lutheran Theological Southern Seminary of LRU before moving to the Lehigh Valley in late 2017 to serve as a first-call pastor in the Evangelical Lutheran Church in America. As a late millennial, I embody many of the nuances this book represents, and am a testament to the ways this entire process can enrich the lives of nones, dones, and the religious faithful of all generations in mutual conversation and relationship.

Sue: Young and thoughtful, reflective and committed, Brandon brings a unique perspective and often challenging insights to our team. While wholly dedicated to the church, he is equally able to be a loving critic and thoughtful problem solver. A millennial himself, he offers a unique perspective and valuable viewpoint. Brandon is tech savvy and my fellow sweet tooth on the team.

Rev. Dr. Joanne P. Marchetto

Joanne: I serve as pastor of The Barn, an innovative church that welcomes people on a spiritual journey. I received my M.Div. and D.Min. degrees from Lancaster Theological Seminary. My doctoral research has focused on the intersection of biblical studies, and sociological and ethnographic research. I am passionate about discovering innovative ways to share our faith stories, learning from others, deepening relationships, and working for social justice in community. My family inspires me, and I give thanks to Jim, Anna, and Jack for their love, support, and ability to play and wonder about God.

Sue: A master juggler of family, ministry, and home, Jo is a high-energy team player who offers very open perspectives and insight. As one both raising and working with youth, she kept us in touch. The pastor of an innovative community, her perspective is invaluable to our work. Her understanding and insight around ethnographic research proved most helpful. Jo is a gifted pastor, teacher, and expresses a prophetic voice as well. She is a great sounding board and processor. Also... our salad connoisseur.

Dr. Jill Peters

Jill: After building a successful rep company in microelectronic sales, I went to graduate school and earned a master's in theology, another in organizational leadership, and a doctorate in ministry in advanced missional leadership. My husband, Rich, has taken over the rep company, which has allowed me to develop a new career in teaching, consulting, and running congregational workshops. My sense of call has always been around encouraging lay people to discover their call and to strengthen congregations. I have accomplished this call through my work through the Crossroads Lay Leadership program at Moravian Theological Seminary. I feel that understanding the emerging generations and how they relate to the traditional church is critical to us building faith communities that welcome, nurture, and serve those inside and outside. For relaxation, I garden, enjoy my fish pond, collect shells, love to watch movies, and spend time with my grandchildren. Being on the team for this book has been one of the joys of my life.

Sue: Jill brings a background in business and organizational leadership, which is very helpful to our work. She represents the voice of those inside and outside the church, which impacted our work. Practical, honest, direct, and loving all describe Jill. The master of juggling 50 balls in the air at the same time, she finds time to do thoughtful work and contribute in meaningful ways. She's also funny! She let us gather in her shore home... so of course we love her.

Stephen Simmons, PhD

Steve: Originally a Midwesterner, I am now a resident of the Lehigh Valley in Pennsylvania. I have pastored congregations in Oregon, Illinois, and Pennsylvania, and, most recently, have taught theology, ethics, and community ministry at Moravian Theological Seminary in Bethlehem. I hold an M.Div. degree from San Francisco Theological Seminary, and a Ph.D. from the University of Chicago, and am ordained in the PCUSA. In retirement, I am an editor for the *International Journal of Practical Theology*, focusing on the intersection between church and culture, particularly as it relates to emerging generations, and on global and interfaith theologies.

Sue: Steve has the incredible ability to take complex, academic theories and articulate them in practical and useful ways. He has a wonderful sense of humor and a knack for timing. He is an avid reader, and we spent half of our book budget adding to his library. Steve is remarkable in his ability to summarize large periods of history in a sentence and transfer that knowledge to everyday life. He loves the church and has a heart for those outside the fold. He's also the most skilled at taking us down rabbit holes.

Janet Stahl

Janet: Born in Bethlehem, Pennsylvania, I devoted my career to cross-cultural work. I have an MA in bilingual multicultural education and have worked as a linguist-translator with Wycliffe Bible Translators in Vanuatu and countries in Asia and Africa. My husband, Jim, and I currently assist teams of minority language speakers to internalize, translate, and tell biblical stories in their often-unwritten languages. The process Jim and I have designed explores the intersection between native traditional stories and the Bible stories to develop their theology. I am drawn to this work to further explore the power of storytelling-in-community in our changing world.

Sue: Thoughtful and inquisitive, dedicated and committed, Janet has dedicated her life in service of God to the world. If more people of faith had her openness and sincerity, we wouldn't have needed to write our book. Janet lives and embodies the storytelling work she and Jim have developed in her everyday life. She is reflective and brings to our team reflective questions and queries. Helping to care for Jim's 95-year-old mother, whose health needs have increased over our time together, she still manages to juggle all her many commitments with love and grace.

James Stahl

Jim: I was born in Bethlehem, Pennsylvania, and currently live there with my wife, Janet. My master's thesis from UT-Arlington was based on qualitative and quantitative research conducted in Kohistan, a northern part of Pakistan. Additionally, I researched sociolinguistic and language development issues in South Asia, the Philippines, and Vanuatu. Since 2006, Janet and I have used a biblical storytelling methodology that helps communities around the world begin Bible translation and engage with scripture in their own languages. As a member of this team, I've been able to draw from experience and expertise in sociolinguistic research, interviewing, and storytelling.

Sue: A man of few (yet thoughtful) words, soft spoken, solid, and articulate, Jim has been a great challenger of our assumptions. His and Janet's global experience and perspective have been invaluable to our team. Jim often asks questions and makes comments that no one else thinks of and yet they are integral to our work. Jim's thoughtful reflections and insights have stretched us all. He's also our coffee man!

Rev. Dr. Sue Pizor Yoder

Sue: I was born in Steeler Territory but married and moved to the Lehigh Valley in Pennsylvania 38 years ago. A pastor of 40 years, I have had the privilege of serving four very large traditional congregations; one small, declining congregation; and planting two new faith communities. My doctoral work explored how each emerging generation is less inclined toward the institutional church and why. I am passionate about researching and partner with others to explore this reality and offer those learnings for reflection and dialogue. I'm a curious, people-loving person by nature, and have had the privilege of doing what I love for 40 years. I "get to" play at my work! I am mother to three amazing adult children, have a wonderful partner of 39 years and love to travel, hike, sing, and cook.

NOTES

PREFACE

1 www.thebarnlv.org

2 www.blankslatecommunity.com

3 Born before 1946, The Greatest Generation receives the alternative moniker "builders" due to their role in laying the foundation for the economic and infrastructural boom experienced in the United States. Builders fought in both world wars, endured the Great Depression, and staffed the various New Deal programs that brought the rural US into the modern age. For more information, see Sue Pizor Yoder, *Preaching to the Whole Household of God: A Homiletic That Speaks to Mixed Generations* (Pittsburgh: 2001).

4 Boomers (people born between 1946 and 1964) are so named because of the large baby boom following the return of American GIs at the end of World War II. In addition to the population spike, boomers enjoyed the fruits of the economic boom established by their builder parents. For more information, see Sue Pizor Yoder, *Preaching to the Whole Household of God: A Homiletic That Speaks to Mixed Generations* (Pittsburgh: 2001).

5 Busters (born between 1965 and 1980) receive their designation in part due to the stark contrast in birth rates among this generation, causing a "baby bust." More commonly referred to as Generation X, busters also participate in busting the cultural expectations of previous generations, a trend started by their boomer predecessors, and continued by millennial and Generation Z successors. For more information, see Sue Pizor Yoder, *Preaching to the Whole Household of God: A Homiletic That Speaks to Mixed Generations* (Pittsburgh: 2001).

INTRODUCTION

1 We have laid out a brief snippet of our desire to facilitate meaningful conversation in our Preface. Never skip the preface, folks! It literally sets up everything.

2 For more information, see *By Any Media Necessary* by Henry Jenkins, et al. and *The Emerging Church, Millennials and Religion* by Randall Reed and Michael G. Zbaraschuk.

3 Jean Twenge and William Keith Campbell, *The Narcissism Epidemic: Living in the Age of Entitlement* (New York: Atria Paperback, 2013), 292.

4 See Henry Jenkins et al., *By Any Media Necessary: The New Youth Activism*, especially 219–52, "Bypassing the Ballot Box: How Libertarian Youth Are Reimagining the Political."

5 Nancy E. Hill and Alexis Redding. "The Real Reason Young Adults Seem Slow to 'Grow Up.'" *The Atlantic*. Last modified April 28, 2021. Accessed June 7, 2022. https://bit.ly/3XsmKui

6 For more information on this, see *Narcissism Epidemic* by Jean Twenge and William Keith Campbell and *Second Mountain* by David Brooks.

7 Jean M. Twenge, *IGen: Why Today's Super-Connected Kids Are Growing up Less Rebellious, More Tolerant, Less Happy—And Completely Unprepared for Adulthood: And What That Means for the Rest of Us* (New York: Atria Books, 2018), 2.

8 Twenge, *IGen*, 175.

9 Suicide rates are at a 30-year high, and social isolation is now an epidemic. See Casper ter Kuile, *The Power of Ritual: Turning Everyday Activities into Soulful Practices* (New York: HarperOne, 2020), 12.

10 Lori Stephens, "The Age of American Despair" (webinar from Harvard Divinity School, Cambridge, MA, March 26, 2020).

11 For more information, see chapter 8 in Twenge, *IGen*.

12 For an extensive assessment of this phenomenon, see Sherry Turkle, *Reclaiming Conversation: The Power of Talk in a Digital Age*. New York: Penguin Press, 2015.

13 See Derek Thompson. "Three Decades Ago, America Lost Its Religion. Why?" *The Atlantic*. Last modified September 26, 2019. Accessed June 7, 2022. https://bit.ly/2nySovt.

14 Twenge, *IGen*, 182.

15 For further information, see chapter 7 of Twenge, *IGen*.

16 Lia M. McIntosh, Jasmine Rose Smothers, and Rodney T. Smothers, *Blank Slate: Write Your Own Rules for a 22nd-Century Church Movement* (Nashville: Abingdon Press, 2019), 47.

17 George Lewis, "LVEDC Board Adopts New Three-Year Strategic Plan and 2022 Budget," Lehigh Valley Economic Development Corporation, December 15, 2021, https://bit.ly/3i6annK, accessed March 21, 2022.

18 "Lehigh Valley Has the Fastest-Growing Young Population in Pennsylvania, Ranging from 18–34-Year-olds," *National Law Review*, vol. XII, no. 326, September 9, 2021, https://bit.ly/3XBAtPQ, accessed March 29, 2022.

19 See Appendix 1 for details about how we adopted the process of ethnographic research.

20 Stories connect us in relationship; when one tells a story, it immediately evokes stories. As we have listened to their stories, we have connected our stories. We also invite you to reflect on your own stories as a part of this conversational process. Stories draw us closer to one another and invite us into relationship.

21 "50 Best Quotes for Storytelling." The Storyteller Agency. https://bit.ly/3hV2Cki, accessed February 28, 2022.

CHAPTER 1

1 Matthew Dickerson and David O'Hara, *Homer to Harry Potter.* (Grand Rapids: Brazos Press, 2006), 35–36.

2 B. Schiff and C. Noy, "Making It Personal: Shared Meanings in the Narratives of Holocaust Survivors," ed. D. Schiffrin and M. Bamberg, A. De Fina. *Discourse and Identity* (Cambridge: Cambridge University Press), 399.

3 B. Schiff and C. Noy, 399.

4 Douglas Adams, *The Prostitute in the Family Tree: Discovering Humor and Irony in the Bible* (Louisville: Westminster John Knox Press, 1997), 6.

5 This story was shared by teenagers in a Sunday school class led by Janet Stahl.

6 Arthur W. Frank, *Letting Stories Breathe: A Socio-narratology* (Chicago: University of Chicago Press, 2010), 40.

7 Arthur Frank, *Letting Stories Breathe,* 34.

8 Arthur Frank, *Letting Stories Breathe,* 34

9 Arthur Frank, *Letting Stories Breathe,* 34–35.

10   Arthur Frank, *Letting Stories Breathe*, 35.

11   Michael Pratt and Barbara Fiese, eds., *Family Stories and the Life Course*. (London: Taylor & Francis Group, 2004), 3.

12   Mike Proulx, *Reaching Gen Z Starts with Understanding Their Truths*. https://bit.ly/3ACNVcf, accessed January 14, 2021.

13   Mike Proulx, *Reaching Gen Z*.

14   Tyler Huckabee, *How GenZ Is Shaping the Church*, Relevant+, https://bit.ly/3i4BRKy, accessed September 6, 2021.

15   "How Gen Z Will Shape the Church" from *The Tide Report*, Springtide Research Institute.

16   "Study Reveals Gen Z as the Loneliest Generation In America." *Addiction Center*. https://bit.ly/3grcwKa, accessed May 26, 2022.

17   Huckabee, *How GenZ Is Shaping the Church*.

CHAPTER 2

1   William B. Bradbury, "Jesus Loves Me," Public Domain.

2   "Maslow's Hierarchy of Needs and Blackfoot (Siksika) Nation Beliefs," - *Rethinking Learning*, March 10, 2019. https://bit.ly/3OBeqVm, accessed June 12, 2022.

3   Sebastian Junger, *Tribe: On Homecoming and Belonging* (New York: Twelve, 2016), 33.

4   Sebastian Junger, *Tribe*, 48.

5   Sebastian Junger, *Tribe*, 87.

6   Sebastian Junger, *Tribe*, 85.

7   For more information on the history of the Lehigh Valley and Bethlehem Steel, see *Stronger than Steel: Forging a Rust Belt Renaissance* by Jeffrey A. Parks (Bethlehem, PA: Rocky Rapids Press, 2018).

8   Personal conversation with Rev. Keith Brown.

9   John Powell, *Why Am I Afraid To Tell You Who I Am?* (London: Fount, 1999), 12.

10   Brené Brown, *Rising Strong*, 158.

11   Grant Skeldon, *The Passion Generation: The Seemingly Reckless, Definitely Disruptive, But Far From Hopeless Millennials* (Grand Rapids: Zondervan, 2018), 29.

12   Lia McIntosh, Jasmine Smothers, and Rodney Thomas Smothers, *Blank Slate: Write Your Own Rules for a 22nd Century Church Movement.* (Nashville: Abingdon Press, 2019), 34.

13   Robert Putnam, 287.

14   Randall Reed and Michael G. Zbaraschuk, eds. *The Emerging Church, Millennials, and Religion: Volume 1: Prospects and Problems* (Eugene, OR: Cascade, 2018), 8.

15   Jean M. Twenge. *IGen: Why Today's Super-Connected Kids Are Growing up Less Rebellious, More Tolerant, Less Happy–and Completely Unprepared for Adulthood–and What That Means for the Rest of Us* (New York: Simon & Schuster, 2018), 50.

16   Twenge, *IGen*, 111.

17   Jane McGonigal, *Imaginable: How to See the Future Coming and Feel Ready for Anything—Even Things That Seem Impossible Today* (New York: Spiegel and Grau, 2022), 135.

18   Twenge, *IGen*, 104.

19   Casper ter Kuile and Angie Thurston. "Something More." Harvard Divinity School and The Fetzer Institute.

20   David Brooks, *The Second Mountain: A Quest for a Moral Life* (New York: Random House, 2019), 31.

21   David Brooks, *The Second Mountain*, 193.

CHAPTER 3

1   Zygmunt Bauman, *Community: Finding Safety in an Insecure World* (Malden, MA: Blackwell Publishing, 2001), 63.

2   Brené Brown, *Atlas of the Heart: Mapping Meaningful Connection and the Language of Human Experience* (New York: Random House, 2021), 77.

3   J. R. R Tolkien, *The Lord of the Rings.* Three-vol. Ed. (Boston: Houghton Mifflin, 2003), xv. As Tolkien said, "I cordially dislike allegory in all its manifestations, and always have done so since I grew old and wary enough to detect its presence. I much prefer history—true or feigned—with its varied applicability to the thought and experience of readers. I think that many confuse applicability with allegory, but the one resides in the freedom of the reader, and the other in the purposed domination of the author."

4   James F. Hopewell, *Congregation: Stories and Structures* (Minneapolis: Fortress Press, 1987), 75.

5   Richard W. Swanson, *Provoking the Gospel: Methods to Embody Biblical Storytelling Through Drama* (Cleveland: Pilgrim Press, 2004), vii.

6   Hopewell cautions, "To use biblical narrative as a descriptive tool by which to picture the local church is to reduce its meaning to that of a companion image, a metaphor that reflects and enriches careful self-understanding. Eviscerated from such a use of the Bible is its prophetic, challenging, always elusive message which often defies self-understanding. The church canonizes the Bible not because it provides a mythical picture of congregations but because it contends with the self-characterizations that Christian households are wont to construct." (Op. cit., 113–14)

In using stories like the myths of Daedalus, Orpheus, and Oedipus, or contemporary stories like *The Godfather* to describe the life of congregations, Hopewell suggests that we can surface their character and values so that they may be subjected to a prophetic critique. Moreover, by engaging in collective storytelling, a congregation may raise up its dynamic and multilayered character in a way that a single image or self-concept can't. "Rather than reduce its self-image to that of a machine or an organism, the congregation might begin to give account of itself as the full, storied household the Bible promises it can be." (Op. cit., 141)

7   Walter J. Ong, S.J., *Orality and Literacy: The Technologizing of the Word* (Oxfordshire, England, UK: Routledge, 1982), 66.

CHAPTER 4

1   Michelle Obama, *Becoming*, 1st ed. (New York: Crown, 2018), 343.

2   "Building Your Resilience." https://www.apa.org/topics/resilience/building-your-resilience, accessed April 4, 2022.

3   "Trauma." n.d. American Psychological Association. Accessed March 11, 2022. https://www.apa.org/topics/trauma.

4   "Why Gen Z Is More Open to Talking About Their Mental Health," Verywell Mind, accessed April 4, 2022, https://bit.ly/3EWCjDE

5   "Why Gen Z Is More Open to Talking About Their Mental Health."

6   Amanda Gorman and Oprah Winfrey, *The Hill We Climb: An Inaugural Poem for the Country* (New York: Viking, 2021).

7   Richard F. Mollica, *Healing Invisible Wounds: Paths to Hope and Recovery in a Violent World.* (Orlando: Harcourt, 2006), 176.

8   Elie Wiesel, *The Gates of the Forest* (New York: Schocken Books, 1996).

9   Elie Wiesel, *Messengers of God: Biblical Portraits and Legends* (New York: Summit Books, 1985).

10   Wiesel, *Messengers of God*, 285.

11   Mollica, *Healing Invisible Wounds*, 176.

12   Mollica, *Healing Invisible Wounds*, 177.

13   Janet Stahl, "Bible Storytelling and Healing Communities," Arts and Faith 5, no. 1 (2017), 11.

14   Stahl, "Bible Storytelling," 7.

15   Stahl, "Bible Storytelling," 115.

16   These interviews took place in November 2020 through March 2021. At the time, there was no vaccine, and there was continued isolation. Many people were working from home, and many schools, colleges, and churches were meeting virtually.

17   Recall the conversation regarding escape in chapter 3 where favorite media can be an escape from reality.

18   Melissa Florer-Bixler, "Why Pastors Are Joining the Great Resignation." *Sojourners.* Last modified November 30, 2021. Accessed March 16, 2022. https://bit.ly/3XntBFB.

19   Florer-Bixler, "Why Pastors Are Joining the Great Resignation."

20   Ryan P. Burge, *The Nones: Where They Came from, Who They Are, and Where They Are Going* (Minneapolis: Fortress Press, 2021).

21   Burge, *The Nones*, 65.

22   If your congregation is struggling with conflict or is struggling in adapting to changes, you can visit https://lmpeacecenter.org/ for more resources.

CHAPTER 5

1   "Definition of LEGACY." Accessed June 9, 2022. https://www.merriam-webster.com/dictionary/legacy.

2   Mary Gormandy White. "What Is a Person's Legacy?" LoveToKnow. Accessed April 11, 2022. https://bit.ly/3Vjez1F.

3   See Joseph Campbell, *The Hero with a Thousand Faces*, 2nd ed. (Novato, CA: New World Library, 2008).

4   Jean M. Twenge and William Keith Campbell. *The Narcissism Epidemic: Living in the Age of Entitlement*. New York: Atria Paperback, 2013.

5   Twenge and Campbell, *The Narcissism Epidemic*, chapter 6.

6   Abridged version of the Good Samaritan, Luke 10.

7   Ursula K. Le Guin, *The Tombs of Atuan*, 1971.

8   Tyndale House Publishers, *Holy Bible: New Living Translation* (Carol Stream, IL: Tyndale House Publishers, 2015), Ec 3:20, 22. Emphasis added.

9   As of August 16, 2022, 71 percent of the Lehigh Valley's two-county population of 664,391 are considered fully vaccinated with at least two doses received. At the same time, 80 percent of that same population has received at least one dose of the vaccine. See statistics for Lehigh and Northampton Counties, PA, at https://bit.ly/3AAACsY, accessed August 16, 2022.

10 Ray Sherman Anderson, *Spiritual Caregiving as Secular Sacrament: A Practical Theology for Professional Caregivers*, Practical Theology Series (London: J. Kingsley Publishers, 2003), 9–10, 174.

11 The word "sacrament" literally means "holy things," and in Protestant traditions most commonly refers to the rituals of Holy Baptism and Holy Communion. Roman Catholics recognize these two sacraments alongside five additional rituals, also considered sacraments. Some expressions of Christianity do not view these as sacraments, but as important rituals prescribed for observation and participation in Christian community and refer to them as ordinances. For more information on these distinctions, see World Council of Churches, *Baptism, Eucharist, and Ministry*, Faith and Order Paper No. 111, World Council of Churches. Geneva, 1982. https://bit.ly/3GCvg44. Accessed July 29, 2022.

12 1 Corinthians 11:24–26 records Jesus's instruction as well as early Christianity's understanding of what this ritual sharing entails. "'This is my body that is for you. Do this in remembrance of me.' In the same way he took the cup also, after supper, saying, 'This cup is the new covenant in my blood. Do this, as often as you drink it, in remembrance of me.' For as often as you eat this bread and drink the cup, you proclaim the Lord's death until he comes." Notice

that while the resurrection event of Easter morning establishes Christianity, Paul encourages that celebrating the Eucharist/Holy Communion is a proclamation of Jesus' *death*. Ritual meal sharing in Christian community is a participatory recollection of Jesus's self-sacrifice, as well as anticipation for this legacy to yield a fuller engagement with the life of the deceased.

13 Stuart Butler and Carmen Diaz, "'Third Places' as Community Builders," September 14, 2016, Brookings, https://brook.gs/3ExfEfr. Accessed April 18, 2022.

14 "Is religion really in decline around the world?" August 27, 2020. Third Space accessed at thirdspace.org.au quoting Ronald Inglehart's article "Giving Up on God: The Global Decline of Religion," *Foreign Affairs*, September-October, 2020.

15 https://www.youtube.com/watch?v=Upm9LnuCBUM   accessed April 18, 2022.

CHAPTER 6

1 Paul Woodruff, *Reverence: Renewing a Forgotten Virtue*, 2nd ed. (New York: Oxford University Press, 2014), 248.

2 In this chapter, the crucified (and now resurrected) Jesus appears to his disciples, all of whom believe that he is, indeed, their risen Lord... except one. Thomas, evidently thinking that his comrades are suffering from some kind of mass delusion, says that he won't believe unless he can actually touch Jesus's wounds. Rather than criticizing Thomas, Jesus invites him to do so; he does, and is convinced. Jesus says, in what is clearly an aside to his first and future disciples, as well as to Thomas, "Do you believe because you have seen? Blessed are those who haven't seen, and yet believe." Jesus doesn't condemn Thomas' skepticism; he accommodates it.

3 John Caputo, *Hoping Against Hope (Confessions of a Postmodern Pilgrim)*, (Minneapolis: Fortress Press, 2015), 39.

4 St. Augustine, *Confessions*, tr. Gary Wills (New York: Penguin Books, 2006), 3-4.

5 Catherine Keller, "The God Perspective," *Tikkun*, July 25, 2014, https://www.tikkun.org/the-god-perspective/, accessed April 14, 2022.

6   Christian Smith, *Soul Searching: The Religious and Spiritual Lives of American Teenagers* (New York: Oxford University Press, 2005), 162–3.

7   Melinda Lundquist Denton and Richard Flory, *Back-Pocket God: Religion and Spirituality in the Lives of Emerging Adults* (New York: Oxford University Press, 2020), eBook, 208.

8   Lundquist Denton and Flory, *Back-Pocket God*, 208.

9   Thomas F. Torrance, *The Trinitarian Faith: The Evangelical Theology of the Ancient Catholic Church* (New York: Bloomsbury Academic, 2016), 135.

10   Ann Christie et al., *Ordinary Christology: Who Do You Say That I Am? Answers from the Pews* (New York: Routledge, 2016), eBook, 41.

11   Woodruff, *Reverence*, 34.

12   Woodruff, *Reverence*, 131.

13   The World Prayer Project. https://bit.ly/3OvExNk, accessed August 2, 2022.

14   For more resources, see Dinner Church Collective at https://dinnerchurch.com/.

CONCLUSION

1   Sue Pizor Yoder, *Preaching to the Whole Household of God: A homiletic that speaks to mixed generations* (Pittsburgh: 2001).

2   Sue Monk Kidd. *The Secret Life of Bees* (New York: Penguin, 2003), 110.

3   Mark Wingfield. "American Young People Report Huge Gaps between What Matters to Them and What Appears to Matter to the Church." *Baptist News Global.* Last modified October 25, 2021. Accessed April 12, 2022. https://bit.ly/3grBgSv.

4   Wingfield, "American Young People."

5   Mike Moore. "The Rise of the 'Umms.'" *Christianity Today.* https://bit.ly/3EqhWx0. Accessed April 2, 2022.

6   Brian D. McLaren. *Faith after Doubt: Why Your Beliefs Stopped Working and What to Do about It*, 1st ed. New York: St. Martin's Essentials, 2021. 134.

7   Ronald Heifetz and Marty Linsky, *Leadership on the Line: Staying Alive Through the Dangers of Leading,* Working Knowledge

(Harvard Business School blog), May 28, 2002, http://hbswk.hbs.edu/archive/2952.html. Accessed January 25, 2022. Quoted in Tod Bolsinger, *Canoeing the Mountains*. InterVarsity Press. Kindle edition.

APPENDIX 1

1   David Kinnaman and Mark Matlock. *Faith for Exiles: 5 Ways for a New Generation to Follow Jesus in Digital Babylon*. Grand Rapids: Baker Books, 2019. 222.

2   Alice Y. Kolb & David A. Kolb. 2013. The Kolb Learning Style Inventory – Version 4.0: A Comprehensive Guide to the Theory, Psychometrics, Research on Validity and Educational Applications. Experience Based Learning Systems, Inc.

APPENDIX 2

1   "US Census Bureau QuickFacts: Lehigh County, Pennsylvania." Accessed April 11, 2022. https://bit.ly/3UoDndT.

2   "US Census Bureau QuickFacts: Northampton County, Pennsylvania." Accessed April 13, 2022. https://bit.ly/3U1TzeG.

3   "DATALV." Accessed April 11, 2022. https://lvpc.org/datalv.html.

4   Ryan P. Burge. *The Nones: Where They Came from, Who They Are, and Where They Are Going*. Minneapolis: Fortress Press, 2021. 129.

BIBLIOGRAPHY

BOOKS

Adams, Douglas. *The Prostitute in the Family Tree: Discovering Humor and Irony in the Bible*. Louisville: Westminster John Knox Press, 1997.

Anderson, Ray Sherman. *Spiritual Caregiving as Secular Sacrament: A Practical Theology for Professional Caregivers*. Practical theology series. London: J. Kingsley Publishers, 2003.

Aronson, Ronald. *Living without God: New Directions for Atheists, Agnostics, Secularists, and the Undecided*. Berkeley, CA: Counterpoint, 2008.

Astley, Jeff. *Ordinary Theology: Looking, Listening, and Learning in Theology*. Explorations in practical, pastoral, and empirical theology. Hants, England: Aldershot, 2002.

St. Augustine. *Confessions*, tr. Gary Wills. New York: Penguin Books, 2006.

Bauman, Zygmunt. *Community: Seeking Safety in an Insecure World*. Malden, MA: Blackwell Publishing, 2001.

Bolsinger, Tod. *Canoeing the Mountains: Christian Leadership in Uncharted Territory*. Downers Grove, IL: InterVarsity Press, 2018.

Boscaljon, Daniel. *Vigilant Faith: Passionate Agnosticism in a Secular World*. Charlottesville, VA: University of Virginia Press, 2013.

Brooks, David. *The Second Mountain: The Quest for a Moral Life*. New York: Random House, 2020.

Brown, Brené. *Atlas of the Heart: Mapping Meaningful Connection and the Language of Human Experience*. New York: Random House, 2021.

———. *Rising Strong: How the Ability to Reset Transforms the Way We Live, Love, Parent, and Lead*. Random House, 2017.

Burge, Ryan P. *The Nones: Where They Came From, Who They Are, and Where They Are Going*. Minneapolis: 1517 Press, 2021.

Campbell, Joseph. *The Hero with a Thousand Faces*, 2nd ed. Novato, CA: New World Library, 2008.

Caputo, John. *Hoping Against Hope (Confessions of a Postmodern Pilgrim)*. Minneapolis: Fortress Press, 2015.

Chopp, Rebecca. *The Power to Speak: Feminism, Language, God.* Wipf and Stock, 2002.

Christie, Ann. *Ordinary Christology: Who Do You Say that I Am? Answers from the Pews.* Oxford: Ashgate Publishing, 2021.

Creasy Dean, Kenda. *Almost Christian: What the Faith of Our Teenagers Is Telling the American Church.* Oxford: Oxford University Press, 2010.

Crosby, John. *Aftermath: Surviving the Loss of God.* New York: Algora Publishing, 2013.

Denton, Melinda Lundquist, and Richard Flory. *Back-Pocket God: Religion and Spirituality in the Lives of Emerging Adults.* New York: Oxford University Press, 2020.

Dickerson, Matthew, and David O'Hara. *Homer to Harry Potter.* Grand Rapids: Brazos Press, 2020.

Drescher, Elizabeth. *Choosing Our Religion: The Spiritual Lives of America's Nones.* New York: Oxford University Press, 2016.

Durkheim, Émile. *The Elementary Forms of Religious Life,* tr. Carol Cosman. New York: Oxford University Press, 2008.

Dyck, Drew. *Generation Ex-Christian: Why Young Adults Are Leaving the Faith... and How to Bring Them Back.* Chicago: Moody Publishers, 2010.

Fitch, David E. *Seven Practices for the Church on Mission.* London, UK: SPCK Publishing, 2018.

Frank, Arthur W. *Letting Stories Breathe: A Socio-Narratology.* Chicago: University of Chicago Press, 2010.

Frazer, S., A. El-Shafei, A.M. Gill. *Reality Check: Being Nonreligious in America.* Cranford, NJ: American Atheists, 2020.

Friedman, Edwin H. *Generation to Generation: Family Process in Church and Synagogue.* The Guilford family therapy series. New York: Guilford Press, 2011.

Fulkerson, Mary McClintock. *Places of Redemption.* New York: Oxford University Press, 2007.

Geertz, Clifford. *The Interpretation of Culture.* New York: Basic Books, 2000.

Gorman, Amanda and Oprah Winfrey. *The Hill We Climb: An Inaugural Poem for the Country.* New York: Viking, 2021.

Gottschall, Jonathan. *The Storytelling Animal: How Stories Make Us Human.* New York: Houghton, Mifflin, Harcourt, 2012.

Hagglund, Martin. *This Life: Secular Faith and Spiritual Freedom.* New York: Knopf Doubleday, 2020.

Hazleton, Lesley. *Agnostic: A Spirited Manifesto.* New York: Penguin, 2017.

Hopewell, James F. *Congregation: Stories and Structures.* Minneapolis: 1517 Press, 1987.

Jenkins, Henry, et al. *By Any Media Necessary: The New Youth Activism.* New York: NYU Press, 2018.

Junger, Sebastian. *Tribe: On Homecoming and Belonging.* New York: Grand Central Publishing, 2016.

Kearney, Richard. *Anatheism: Returning to God after God.* New York: Columbia University Press, 2011.

Kidd, Sue Monk. *The Secret Life of Bees.* Kindle ed. New York: Penguin Books, 2003.

Kinnaman, David. *You Lost Me: Why Young Christians Are Leaving the Church... and Rethinking Faith.* Grand Rapids: Baker Books, 2011.

Kinnaman, David, and Mark Matlock. *Faith for Exiles: 5 Ways for a New Generation to Follow Jesus in Digital Babylon.* Grand Rapids: Baker Books, 2019.

Kolb, Alice Y., and David A. Kolb. *The Kolb Learning Style Inventory – Version 4.0: A Comprehensive Guide to the Theory, Psychometrics, Research on Validity and Educational Applications.* Kaunakakai, HI: Experience Based Learning Systems, 2013.

Le Guin, Ursula K. *The Tombs of Atuan.* New York: Atheneum Books, 2012.

Luhrmann, T.M. *When God Talks Back: Understanding the American Evangelical Relationship with God.* New York: Knopf Doubleday, 2012.

———. *How God Becomes Real: Kindling the Presence of Invisible Others.* Princeton: Princeton University Press, 2020.

McGonigal, Jane. *Imaginable: How to See the Future Coming and Feel Ready for Anything—Even Things That Seem Impossible Today.* New York: Spiegel and Grau, 2022.

McIntosh, Lia, Jasmine Rose Smothers, Rodney Thomas Smothers. *Blank Slate: Write Your Own Rules for a 22nd-Century Church Movement.* Nashville: Abingdon Press, 2019.

McLaren, Brian D. *Faith after Doubt: Why Your Beliefs Stopped Working and What to Do about It,* 1st. ed. New York: St. Martin's Essentials, 2021.

Mercadante, Linda. *Belief without Borders: Inside the Minds of the Spiritual but Not Religious.* Oxford: Oxford University Press, 2014.

Merritt, Jonathan. *Learning to Speak God from Scratch: Why Sacred Words Are Vanishing—and How We Can Revive Them.* New York: Crown Publishing Group, 2018.

Mollica, Richard F. *Healing Invisible Wounds: Paths to Hope and Recovery in a Violent World.* Orlando, FL: Harcourt, 2006.

Mueller, Sabrina. *Lived Theology: Impulses for a Pastoral Theology of Empowerment.* Eugene, OR: Cascade Books, 2021.

Obama, Michelle. *Becoming,* 1st ed. New York: Crown, 2018.

Ong, Walter J., S.J. *Orality and Literacy: The Technologizing of the Word.* Oxfordshire: Routledge, 1982.

Ozment, Katherine. *Grace without God: The Search for Meaning, Purpose, and Belonging in a Secular Age.* New York: Harper Collins, 2016.

Parks, Jeffrey A. *Stronger than Steel: Forging a Rust Belt Renaissance.* Bethlehem, PA: Rocky Rapids Press, 2018.

Powell, John. *Why Am I Afraid to Tell You Who I Am? Insights into Personal Growth.* London: Fount, 1999.

Pratt, Michael and Barbara Fiese, eds. *Family Stories and the Life Course.* London: Taylor & Francis Group, 2004.

Putnam, Robert D. *Bowling Alone: The Collapse and Revival of American Community.* 1. Touchstone ed. London: Simon & Schuster, 2001.

Reed, Randall, and Michael G. Zbaraschuk, eds. *The Emerging Church, Millennials, and Religion: Volume 1: Prospects and Problems.* Eugene, OR: Cascade, 2018.

Rendle, Gilbert R. *Leading Change in the Congregation: Spiritual and Organizational Tools for Leaders.* Bethesda, MD.: Alban Institute, 1998.

Ritchie, Donald A. *Doing Oral History: A Practical Guide,* 2nd ed. NY: Oxford, 2003.

Rushkoff, Douglas. *Nothing Sacred: The Truth about Judaism.* New York: Crown/Archetype, 2004.

Sayers, Dorothy. *Letters to a Diminished Church: Passionate Arguments for the Relevance of Christian Doctrine.* Nashville: Harper Collins Christian Publishing, 2004.

Schiff, B., and C. Noy. "Making It Personal: Shared Meanings in the Narratives of Holocaust Survivors," in D. Schiffrin, M. Bamberg, and

A. De Fina, ed., *Discourse and Identity.* Cambridge: Cambridge University Press.

Schmidt, Eric, and Eric Rosenberg. *How Google Works.* New York: Grand Central Publishing, 2017.

Seel, David John, Jr. *The New Copernicans: Millennials and the Survival of the Church.* Nashville: Thomas Nelson, 2018.

Skeldon, Grant. *The Passion Generation: The Seemingly Reckless, Definitely Disruptive, But Far From Hopeless Millennials.* Nashville: Harper Collins Christian Publishing/Zondervan, 2018.

Smith, Christian. *Religion: What It Is, How It Works, and Why It Matters.* Princeton: Princeton University Press, 2017.

Smith, Christian, Kari Christofferson, Hilary Davidson, Patricia Snell Herzog. *Lost in Transition: The Dark Side of Emerging Adulthood.* New York: Oxford University Press, 2011.

Smith, Christian, with Melinda Lundquist. *Soul Searching: The Religious and Spiritual Lives of American Teenagers.* New York: Oxford University Press, 2005.

Smith, Christian, with Patricia Snell. *Souls in Transition: The Religious and Spiritual Lives of Emerging Adults.* New York: Oxford University Press, 2009.

Smith, James K.A. *How (Not) to Be Secular: Reading Charles Taylor.* Grand Rapids, MI: William B. Eerdmans, 2014.

Springtide Research Institute. *The State of Religion and Young People: Relational Authority* (2020).

Stahl, Janet. "Biblical Storytelling and Healing Communities." *Arts and Faith* 5, no. 1 (2017).

Staniforth, Nate. *Here is Real Magic.* London: Bloomsbury, 2018.

Stark, David. *Reaching Millennials: Proven Methods for Engaging a Younger Generation.* Grand Rapids: Baker Publishing Group, 2016.

Stark, Rodney, and Roger Finke. *Acts of Faith: Explaining the Human Side of Religion.* Berkeley: University of California Press, 2000.

Steffen, Tom, and William Bjoraker. *The Return of Oral Hermeneutics.* Eugene, OR: Wipf & Stock, 2020.

Steinke, Peter L. *Healthy Congregations: A Systems Approach,* 2nd ed. Herndon, VA: Alban Institute, 2006.

Swanson, Richard W. *Provoking the Gospel: Methods to Embody Biblical Storytelling Through Drama.* Cleveland: Pilgrim Press, 2004.

Swinton, John, and Harriet Mowat. *Practical Theology and Qualitative Research*, 2nd ed. Norwich, UK: Hymns Ancient & Modern Ltd, 2016.

Swinton, John, and Ray Sherman Anderson. *Spiritual Caregiving as Secular Sacrament*. Philadelphia: Jessica Kingsley Publishers, 2003.

ter Kuile, Caspar. *The Power of Ritual: Turning Everyday Activities into Soulful Practices*. New York: Harper Collins, 2020.

Tolkien, J.R.R. *The Fellowship of the Ring*. New York: Random House, 1986.

Torrance, Thomas F. *The Trinitarian Faith: The Evangelical Theology of the Ancient Catholic Church*. New York: Bloomsbury Academic, 2016.

Turkle, Sherry. *Reclaiming Conversation: The Power of Talk in a Digital Age*. New York: Penguin Press, 2015.

Twenge, Jean. *iGen: Why Today's Super-Connected Kids Are Growing Up Less Rebellious, More Tolerant, Less Happy—and Completely Unprepared for Adulthood—and What That Means for the Rest of Us*. New York: Simon and Schuster/Atria Books, 2017.

Twenge, Jean, and William Keith Campbell. *The Narcissism Epidemic: Living in the Age of Entitlement*. New York: Simon and Schuster/Atria Books, 2010.

Warnell, Jessica McManus. *Engaging Millennials for Ethical Leadership: What Works for Young Professionals and Their Managers*. Singapore: Business Expert Press, 2015.

Webber, Robert E. *The Younger Evangelicals: Facing the Challenges of the New World*. Grand Rapids: Baker Publishing Group, 2002.

White, James Emery. *The Rise of the Nones: Understanding and Reaching the Religiously Unaffiliated*. Grand Rapids: Baker Books, 2014.

Wiesel, Elie. *Messengers of God: Biblical Portraits and Legends*. New York: Summit Books, 1985.

———. *The Gates of the Forest*. New York: Schocken Books, 1996.

Woo, Rodney M. *The Color of Church: A Biblical and Practical Paradigm for Multiracial Churches*. Nashville: B&H Publishing Group, 2003.

Woodruff, Paul. *Reverence: Renewing a Forgotten Virtue*, 2nd ed. New York: Oxford University Press, 2014.

Yoder, Sue Pizor. *Preaching to the Whole Household of God: A homiletic that speaks to mixed generations*. Pittsburgh: 2001.

Zuckerman, Phil. *Living the Secular Life: New Answers to Old Questions.* New York: Penguin, 2015.

ARTICLES

"50 Best Quotes for Storytelling." The Storyteller Agency. Accessed February 28, 2022. https://bit.ly/3VoFutb.

"Building Your Resilience." https://www.apa.org/topics/resilience/building-your-resilience. Accessed April 4, 2022.

Butler, Stewart M., and Carmen Diaz. "Third Places as Community Builders," Brookings Institution, September 14, 2016. https://brook.gs/3Ev300K. Accessed April 18, 2022

"Definition of LEGACY." https://www.merriam-webster.com/dictionary/legacy. Accessed June 9, 2022.

Florer-Bixler, Melissa. "Why Pastors Are Joining the Great Resignation." *Sojourners.* Last modified November 30, 2021. https://bit.ly/3ERfJw3, accessed March 16, 2022.

Griffith, Erin. "Why Are Young People Pretending to Love Work?" *New York Times,* January 26, 2019. https://nyti.ms/2Sdr7dY.

Hill, Nancy E. and Alexis Redding. "The Real Reason Young Adults Seem Slow to 'Grow Up.'" *The Atlantic.* Last modified April 28, 2021. https://bit.ly/3OtVkQM accessed June 7, 2022.

Huckabee, Tyler. *How GenZ Is Shaping the Church.* Relevant+, https://relevantmagazine.com/magazine/how-gen-z-will-shape-the-church/, accessed September 6, 2021.

Keller, Catherine. "The God Perspective," *Tikkun,* July 25, 2014, https://bit.ly/3gpIUNt, accessed April 14, 2022.

"Lehigh Valley Has the Fastest-Growing Young Population in Pennsylvania, Ranging from 18–34-Year-olds," *National Law Review,* vol. XII, no. 326, September 9, 2021, https://bit.ly/3XBAtPQ, accessed March 29, 2022.

Lewis, George. "LVEDC Board Adopts New Three-Year Strategic Plan and 2022 Budget," Lehigh Valley Economic Development Corporation, December 15, 2021, https://bit.ly/3Vk6j1v, accessed March 21, 2022.

Mocek, Christian. "Millennial Philanthropy Can Teach Catholic Church Three Things," *National Catholic Reporter,* April 19, 2018, https://bit.ly/3OttDHL.

Nemeroff, Charles B., and Christine Heim. n.d. "Neurobiology of Post-traumatic Stress Disorder." *CNS Spectrums* 14 (1 Supplement).

Oaklander, Mandy. "Bounce Back: Scientists Now Know Why Some People Rebound So Well From Setbacks." *Time*, May 21, 2005, p. 38.

O'Malley, Alison L. and Denise E. Williams O'Malley. "Emerging Leaders: The Roles of Flourishing and Spirituality in Millennials' Leadership Development Activity," (2012) Journal of Spirituality, Leadership, and Management, 6 (2012), 48–58. https://bit.ly/3XkJUmF.

Proulx, Mike. *Reaching Gen Z Starts with Understanding Their Truths.* https://bit.ly/3TXXIAj, accessed Jan 14, 2021.

"Religion Among the Millennials" (Washington, DC: Pew Research Center, 2010), https://pewrsr.ch/3TU4nf7.

Stein, Joel. "The Subscription Box That Teaches Kids to Do Good," *New York Times*, June 19, 2021.

Thompson, Derek. "Three Decades Ago, America Lost Its Religion. Why?" *The Atlantic*. Last modified September 26, 2019. https://bit.ly/2nySovt, accessed June 7, 2022.

"Trauma." n.d. American Psychological Association, https://www.apa.org/topics/trauma, accessed March 11, 2022.

Verywell Mind. "Why Gen Z Is More Open to Talking About Their Mental Health," https://bit.ly/3tQ3pWD, accessed April 4, 2022.

"When Americans Say They Believe in God, What Do They Mean?", Pew Forum, April 25, 2018, https://pewrsr.ch/3U4JOfU.

White, Mary Gormandy "What Is a Person's Legacy?" LoveToKnow, https://bit.ly/3EyHesH, accessed April 11, 2022.

"The Age Gap in Religion Around the World." Pew Forum, June 13, 2018, https://pewrsr.ch/3Xpy6PX.

"Study Reveals Gen Z as the Loneliest Generation In America." *Addiction Center*, https://bit.ly/3Xp8RgA, accessed May 26, 2022.

WEBINARS

Lori Stephens, "The Age of American Despair," (webinar from Harvard Divinity School, Cambridge, MA, March 26, 2020).

Spirituality and Personality Type resources:

Spiritual Practices' "Spirituality for Your Personality Type" can lead to new insights about their own approach to spiritual discipline: (http://spiritualpractice.ca/what_practice/type/).

www.insights.com for DISC inventory